Stained Gla
Stitchery Bowls

GAIL LAWTHER

TEAMWORK
CRAFTBOOKS

Contents

Where did it all begin? 4

What will I use my bowls for? 5

What stuff do I need? 7

Assembling the bowls 10

Over to you ... 14

THE COLLECTIONS

The Flower Garden 15
Marigold 16
Periwinkle 17
Black-Eyed Susan 18
Primula 19
Templates 20

Christmas Treats 21
Midnight Stars 22
Poinsettia 23
The Heart of Christmas 24
Doves of Peace 25
Gingerbread Men 26
Templates 27

Easter Eggs Etcetera 29
Bright Easter Eggs 30
Embroidered Eggs 31
Easter Basket 32
Asymmetric Flower 33
Templates 34

The Seaside Collection 35
Nautilus Shells 36
Starfish 37
Scallops 38
Tropical Fish 39
Under the Sea 40
Templates 41

The Great Outdoors 43
Green Leaves 44
Mushrooms 45
St Clement's 46
Flower Basket 47
Templates 48

The Chinese Collection 50
Plum Blossom 51
Fans 52
Oriental Clouds 53
Butterflies 54
Ginger Jars 55
Templates 56

Jacobean Jewels 58
Embroidered Flower 59
Tulips 60
Carnation 61
Pomegranates 62
Templates 63

Fields and Hedgerows 64

Primrose 65

Campion 66

Briar Rose 67

Poppy 68

Templates 69

Art Deco Delights 70

Embroidered Triangle 71

Curved Square 72

Wavy Square 73

Pentagon Flower 74

Asymmetric Pentagon 75

Templates 76

Kids' Stuff 78

Bright Flowers 79

Rainbow Hexagon 80

Teddies 81

Duck-Pond 82

Long Basket 83

Templates 84

The Exotic Collection 86

Blazing Sun 87

Pointed Flower 88

Braided Bowl 89

Scalloped Flower 90

Templates 91

Base and centre templates 92

Basic bowl templates 95

Contact details 96

hexagon base
H

Stained Glass Stitchery Bowls
First published in 2007 by
Teamwork Craftbooks

Text, illustration, photographs and
bowl designs © Gail Lawther
unless otherwise indicated

*Our thanks to Tim Bell, for his expertise
in taking all the styled photographs*
www.photobell.com

The designs, projects, illustrations and
other material in this book may not be
used for workshops without obtaining
prior permission (in writing) from
the author.

ISBN 978 0 9553499 2 8
British Library Cataloguing in Publication Data
A catalogue record for this book is available
from the British Library

Designed and created by Teamwork,
Christopher and Gail Lawther,
44 Rectory Walk, Sompting, Lancing,
West Sussex, England BN15 0DU
thelawthers@ntlworld.com

Set in ITC Legacy Sans & ITC Tiepolo

Printed by Patersons Total Print Solutions,
Tunbridge Wells, Kent (www.patersons.com)

Where did it all begin?

WHEN I was making the bowls featured in this book, I found it hard to limit myself to 50 designs: each one I did sparked off several more ideas in my brain! But, I hear you ask – where did all of these ideas come from? What on earth started me along this path in the first place?!

Several years ago I saw a couple of books by Linda Johansen on creating simple bowls from fabric. I was intrigued by the idea of using textiles to create 3D objects, but felt that making the bowl from just one piece of fabric rather limited the shapes and effects you could achieve. I bought some interfacing and began experimenting with different shapes and ideas. The first bowl I made was a sunflower shape for my book *Stained Glass Patchwork Techniques* (above); on this design, each petal is made from a different yellow print fabric, stitched around a brown centre. My husband Chris and I had this bowl on our table when we were demonstrating at the Festival of Quilts at NEC, and so many people were fascinated by it that I began to play around with the idea a bit more.

A trip to the city of Napier in New Zealand inspired all kinds of Art Deco ideas in my quilting work, and one of these was a bowl based on Art Deco architectural shapes (right), which I did as a project for *Fabrications* magazine. More interest: so when I

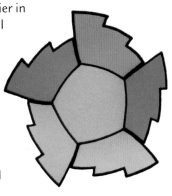

was working on *Fun and Fabulous Patchwork and Appliqué* for David & Charles, I made a couple of flower bowls in the shapes of daisies (right) and anemones (below). These led to still more intrigue, more people wanting to know how they were done, and yet more ideas for bowl shapes. Eventually I bowed to the inevitable and realised that I was going to have to put all these ideas in a book!

The results are the 50 different bowl designs that I've included in this book. In the first section I've covered the basics that you need to know to create the designs – the (very simple) equipment that you need, and how to work with the interfacing and construct a couple of basic bowls. Then the designs are divided into collections by theme; each individual bowl has complete step-by-step instructions, and all the templates for all the bowls are full size and ready to use. Some of the bowls use the same base template; we've put all the standard base templates at the end of the book, to make them easy to find.

I've also given each design an easiness rating; the more the stars, the more challenging the design is. Although every stitcher is different in how quickly or slowly they work, you can also use the stars as a very rough indication of how many hours a bowl will take – so for instance the Plum Blossom design on page 51 has two stars, so it should take you somewhere around two hours to create it. You'll find that once you make a few of these bowls they become addictive: like me, you'll think of different ways in which you can adapt and embellish or vary them. And if you run out of ideas, don't worry: I've got designs for at least another 50 running round in my head!

What will I use my bowls for?

I can picture you saying, 'OK: I've already got loads of ideas for making bowls. I like the look of the oranges and lemons, and I fancy making one like a primrose – and I love the attitude of the gingerbread men. I'm all set to get on a roll and make dozens of these bowls, but what am I going to put in them?!' Well, I've got loads of ideas, and I bet these will give you lots more.

- As I live near the seaside, let's begin with some of the things you find there. Shells, stones (polished ones look particularly good), fossils, starfish, sand-dollars, glass blobs.

- Jewellery – serious baubles, costume jewellery, and kids' endless bracelets and rings. Make a bowl you can use to keep your rings safe while you're washing up or washing your hair.

- Hair bits and pieces; make a special little girl her own bowl for keeping her hair slides, clips, ribbons and scrunchies tidy.

- How about sweets and snacks? Obviously you don't want to fill your bowl with gooey chunks of fudge (though see the note on page 9 about washing), but these bowls are wonderful showcases for wrapped sweets of all kinds. Try easter eggs, chocolate coins, sugared almonds, After Eights, toffees, fruit drops, humbugs, glacier mints etc, as well as mixed foil-wrapped chocolates and those little fun-sized bars of chocolate. (Although as Jasper Carrot once commented: if you've got a tiny bar of chocolate instead of a large one, where's the fun in that?!) Walnuts, pecans, brazil nuts and pistachios in their shells look good, too.

- Don't forget the men in your life; a nice masculine-looking fabric bowl makes a great place for storing a watch, favourite golf tees, or all that loose change from his pocket each night.

- Kids have endless little bits and pieces, and a series of brightly-coloured bowls in funky fabrics is a good way of encouraging a bit of order amid the chaos! Little toys, marbles, pencils and rubbers, dolls' accessories, tiny teddies, bouncy balls and building bricks.

- When you have an overnight guest, why not leave them a little bowl full of pampering products? Bath salts or sachets of bath oil or shower gel, a tube of foot scrub or moisturiser, a decorative bar of soap, a new flannel. And in your own bathroom, where else can you keep those spare electric toothbrush heads, and those little humming-bird things you're supposed to send on exploratory missions between your teeth?

- It's nice to have something special to hold bits and pieces in the nursery; make a bowl in bright or pastel colours and make sure that you always have some cotton buds, cotton-wool balls and wrapped baby wipes ready to hand. I made one of these for a friend's baby shower, and filled it with practical things like earplugs and paracetamol ...

- If you're lucky enough to have a conservatory or potting shed, make a series of bowls for holding plant ties, seed packets, balls of twine, seed sticks etc. If you haven't got a special room, make a bowl or two to serve the same purpose on the kitchen windowsill – or for the cupboard under the stairs.

- Christmas wouldn't be Christmas without some chocolate coins and brightly-striped candy sticks; show them off in a seasonal bowl. Pine-cones or walnuts sprayed gold or silver look good, too and you can also use your bowls to show off little baubles.

- Natural materials can be set off very well by printed fabrics: driftwood, wooden eggs, pine-cones, seed cases, skeleton leaves, acorns. And stitched bowls are a gift for pot pourri and dried flowers; a bowl of dried lavender or rose petals smells much nicer than a synthetic air freshener.

- And don't forget the kitchen; use some of your bowls for storing all those funny little items that don't have any other home! You know the ones: corn-on-the-cob forks, chopstick rests, cocktail sticks ...

- In the office or study, keep rubbers, paper clips, elastic bands, stapler (and staples), pencil sharpener etc corralled where you can always find them.

- You're already a stitcher, so you're probably surrounded by reels of thread, skeins of embroidery cotton, thimbles, marking tools, buttons and charms, packs of needles and pins, containers of beads etc. A stitched bowl is a pretty and practical way of keeping bits and pieces in one place while you're working on a project.

What will I use my bowls for?

What stuff do I need?

Equipment

The one piece of equipment that's vital for stitching these bowls is a sewing machine: the exact make and type doesn't matter, as long as it does zigzag. You need very little other equipment, and my guess is that you've already got everything you need in your basic sewing kit.

- scissors: paper scissors, good-quality fabric-cutting scissors, and small sharp-pointed embroidery scissors
- soft pencil
- long pins (these are useful for holding the sections of the bowl together securely while you stitch them)
- chalk marker
- long quilt rule
- felt pens (see page 13!)
- paper
- template plastic or thin card for making templates (optional)

That was pretty painless, wasn't it?

Threads

The thread you use to edge your patches is an important part of the design. Because I wanted to give my bowls a stained glass effect, I picked out for each one a thread colour that contrasted strongly with the fabric patches I was using. By experimenting, I discovered that it works best if you edge each petal with a double layer of satin stitch. As you can see from the photographs here, a single layer of satin stitch tends to leave a few fibres of fabric showing through the stitching (**a**); when you add a second circuit of satin stitch, though, the result is a really attractive, smooth line of stitching (**b**). If you're not sure exactly how a particular thread choice will work, hold the spool against each of your fabrics in turn; if you're still not quite sure, try a sample of satin stitch out on one of your interfacing offcuts.

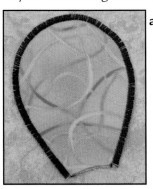 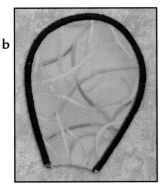

a

b

When you're thinking about threads for stitching your bowls, there's one main factor you need to bear in mind: they use a lot! Because you're working in satin stitch, and stitching round each shape twice, you'll get through a large amount of thread. It's better to buy one large reel of thread than several small ones; that way won't have to keep stopping in the middle of a line of stitching to swap spools. For similar reasons, it's a good trick to wind two or three bobbins in the colour you're using before you begin stitching each bowl: then if your bobbin runs out you can keep the needle threaded, which makes the interruption in the bobbin thread less noticeable.

Different types of thread all have their benefits for this kind of work. Ordinary cotton thread works well and gives a good coverage, but is slightly thicker than other types: if your satin stitch tends to get caught up on itself, you may well find that a slightly finer thread gives you better results. Polyester threads and cotton/polyester mixes are good choices; they're sometimes cheaper than cottons, but still give good coverage. Rayon machine threads have a lovely sheen, and produce a beautifully smooth satin stitch, but they tend to be finer than cottons so you might need to reduce your stitch length slightly to ensure that you cover the fabric well.

Because you need the same thread in the bobbin as you have in the top, metallic threads aren't particularly good for this technique – metallics don't usually behave well as bobbin threads. If you definitely want a thread with a sheen for a particular bowl, try a rayon machine embroidery thread; to edge the patches on the Midnight Stars bowl, shown in the detail here, I used a tan-coloured rayon thread, which looks almost gold against the fabrics.

There are some lovely variegated machine threads on the market, and some of these can work well on bowls. I prefer the threads that change colour at random intervals; the ones that change regularly are a bit too mechanical, and also don't produce a particularly attractive effect when you go round the patches for the second time. I used a variegated thread in soft mid-pastels for edging the Asymmetric Pentagon bowl on page 75.

Fabrics

If you're already a quilter, chances are that most of the fabrics in your stash are cotton; you'll find that these produce excellent results on your bowls. Totally plain or solid colours work well for some of the designs, especially if you want them to look realistic; I used solids for the Campion (page 66), the Primrose (page 65), and the Briar Rose (page 67). Sometimes plains look a bit – well – plain, though, so I also like using lots of mottled, batik and random-dyed fabrics; these create plenty of visual interest while not looking too distracting on small patches. I used these on bowls such as the Pentagon Flower (see page 74), the Primula (page 19), the Tropical Fish (page 39), and the Poppy (page 68). Tiny or subtle prints work well, too, for instance the fern/seaweed print on the Nautilus Shells bowl on page 36, and the three different red fabrics in the Poinsettia (page 23).

If you're using stronger fabric designs or novelty prints, use them for some of the larger or less complex shapes such as the Bright Easter Eggs (page 30), the Heart of Christmas bowl (page 24), or the Long Basket (page 83). Remember that if your print is strongly directional, or you want a motif to appear in a particular alignment on your patches, you may have to adjust the dimensions of your fabric and interfacing strips; if you're not sure, cut several paper duplicates of the relevant template and position them on your fabric to check the layout.

I also like using silk fabrics on these bowls, particularly on the Jacobean designs (see pages 58-62). If you fancy trying silk, use dupions; they are more firmly woven than other silks, and are much easier to work with. For the Scalloped Flower on page 90, I used a rich embroidered silk. Other firm fabrics such as some polyesters and satins may also work well; try them out on offcuts of interfacing, and also check that you can use the iron to fuse them without any problems.

Metallic fabrics are worth experimenting with, too; some of them don't take very kindly to being ironed, so try out sample pieces first of all. If the fabric has a tendency to stick, use a non-stick sheet between the fabric and the iron while you're doing the fusing. I used a multicoloured metallic fabric for the fish on the Under the Sea bowl on page 40. Sheer fabrics (of any fibre) don't tend to work well on the bowls, as they leave some of the adhesive exposed, but you may find that you can layer patches of sheer fabrics and then secure them with a pattern of random stitching, similar to the way I've decorated the fabric strip for the Easter Basket on page 32.

You can see from the photographs on this page just how different the same bowl design can look, simply by varying the combination of fabric and thread (**a** and

a

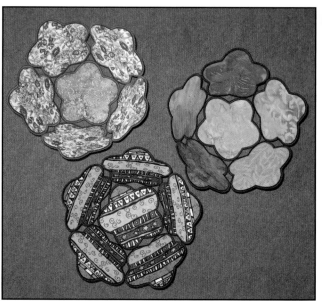

b

b), and there are many other ways in which you can vary the way you use fabrics. For instance, if the design has a suitable number of sides, you can alternate two or three fabrics around the bowl (**c**). On the Long Basket (page 83), I've used one fabric on the outside of the bowl sides and another on the inside. When I was showing the Long Basket to an embroidery group, someone asked whether it was possible to turn it inside out so that the other fabric showed? I wasn't sure, so suggested that we tried it out! And the answer was, yes, you can (see photographs **d** and **e**). Two bowls for the price of one ... what more could you want?

c

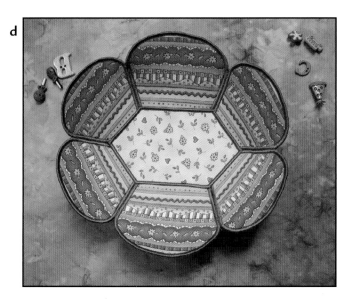

d

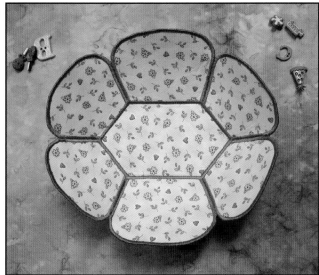

e

You can also use a different fabric or print for each petal of a flower or side of a bowl; I've done this on bowls such as the Asymmetric Flower (page 33), Green Leaves (page 44), Bright Flowers (page 79) and Ginger Jars (page 55). For the Rainbow Hexagon bowl on page 80, I edged each side piece using the next colour in the spectrum.

For some of the designs in this book, you may find that you want to use your fabrics differently from the way I've stitched the sample – for instance, you might want to do each duck round the Duck-Pond (see page 82) in a different fabric, rather than making them all the same as I've done. For most of the bowls I've provided two options: Option A gives you the materials and instructions for cutting all the side shapes from the same fabric, while Option B provides alternative measurements and instructions for you to follow if you want to cut each shape from a different fabric.

Interfacing

All of the bowls in this book are made by fusing fabric over a firm-yet-flexible interfacing, which is soft enough for you to stitch it while also being stiff enough to create the bowl shape without it collapsing into a heap of fabric. When I made my first bowls (see page 4), I used Timtex ™ as the stiffener; Timtex isn't adhesive, so I had to use bonding web to fuse the fabrics onto the interfacing strips. After I'd made a few, though, I was introduced to Fast2Fuse ™, and there was no looking back!

Fast2Fuse is made by C&T in America, and comes in two versions: one is fusible on one side, but the type you want for these bowls is fusible on both sides. This cuts out the whole bonding web process, which means that your interfacing can be prepared ready for cutting in just a minute or two. It's very easy to work with, and very easy to stitch through. Intriguingly, the manufacturers say on the blurb that it's washable, but I haven't put this to the test. Useful to know, though, in case your bowl gets the odd mark from sticky fingers.

For suppliers of Fast2Fuse, see page 96. It comes in a 10yd bolt, in a standard width of 28in (71cm), and is usually sold by the metre; as a rough guide, one metre of the interfacing will be enough for 8 or 9 of the simple bowls shown on page 11. You can also buy it in 15in (38cm) squares from some suppliers, and in packs; these shapes are a little more limiting than buying it by the metre, as you end up with various offcuts in strange shapes and sizes.

You may have your own favourite interfacing that you'd like to try; the best thing to do is simply try a bit out with the fusing and satin stitch; then, if it seems to work well, try a simple bowl and see how it performs.

In the list of requirements for each bowl I've usually given the 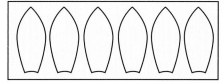 a

dimensions of the interfacing piece you'll need if you're making all the sides of a bowl out of a single strip. Generally these allow you to mark out all the bowl sides or petal shapes in a row (**a**). If you don't have a long strip of interfacing, though, you can simply halve the length and double the width to produce a rectangle, and mark the sides/petals in two batches as shown (**b**). 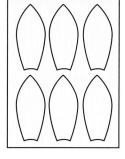 b

Assembling the bowls

IN this section I'll show you the basic method used for assembling a simple flower bowl. If you're new to bowl-making, I suggest that you try this design first; while you're assembling it, you'll learn virtually everything you need to know for producing the other designs in the book, which are either put together in exactly the same way, or are simple variations on this basic sequence. The exact method for each bowl is explained in detail under its individual instructions.

The shapes that make up each bowl are edged with machine satin stitch in a contrasting colour (or colours). I've found by trial and error that two layers of satin stitch create a much better effect than one; after a single circuit of satin stitch there are often still some hairy 'moustaches,' or fabric fibres, showing through the stitching, but once you've gone round the shape twice, you have a firmer and more attractive edging (see page 7). There are various tips to help you create a really good satin stitch; these are mentioned on page 12, where I talk about setting up the stitch on your sewing machine.

Making a basic bowl

For this demonstration I'll use Option A – making each petal from the same fabric.

1 For the petals, cut a 19 x 4in (48 x 10cm) strip of interfacing, and two strips of cotton fabric the same size. Lay a strip of fabric right side up on one side of the interfacing strip; using your iron on the normal setting for cotton, fuse the fabric into place with a warm iron (**a**). (If you do this fairly quickly, you should find that the heat doesn't penetrate through to the other adhesive side of the interfacing!) Turn the

interfacing over, and fuse the second strip of fabric to the other side in the same way. Press both sides well to ensure that the fabric has stuck thoroughly.

2 Trace or photocopy the basic flower template on page 95 and cut it out; using soft pencil, trace round the template to mark six petal shapes (**b**). Cut out the shapes with sharp scissors, cutting along the marked lines (**c**).

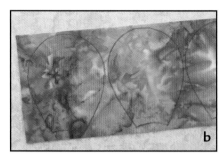

3 For the centre of the flower, cut a 3in (7.5cm) square of interfacing and two matching squares of cotton fabric, and prepare the patch in the same way by fusing a fabric square onto each side of the interfacing (**d**). Now trace or photocopy the centre template from page 95 and cut it out; position it on the prepared patch and trace round it in pencil (**e**), then cut it out (**f**).

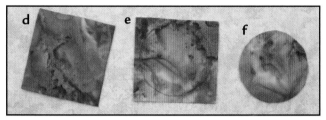

4 Now stitch two layers of satin stitch around the curved edges of the petals (**g**); don't stitch across the bottom edges of the petal shapes yet.

5 Lay the centre circle on a flat surface and arrange the petals evenly around it; the petals should just touch each other, and will tuck slightly under the edges of the centre. I find it useful to do this bit on a rotary-

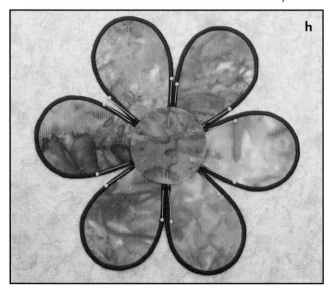

cutting board; the grid helps me position the petals evenly. Use long pins to pin the petals firmly in place; push the pins through the stitching at the edges of the petals, then horizontally into the centre shape as shown (**h**) – this keeps the work nice and rigid, which helps to prevent the petals from shifting out of position while you move them to the machine and stitch them in place.

6 Work two circuits of medium zigzag round the edge of the central circle to secure the petals (**i**), then turn the bowl over and trim the bottoms of the petals on the back of the work if necessary (**j**). Now set your machine for satin stitch again, and work two circuits of satin stitch round the edge of the central circle (**k**).

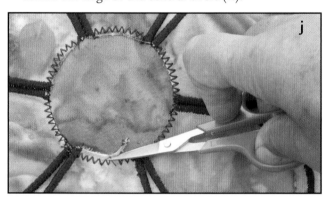

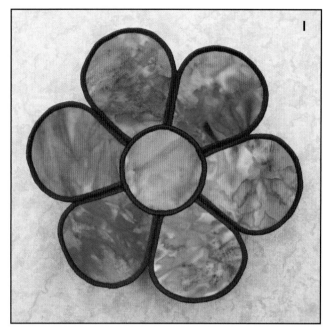

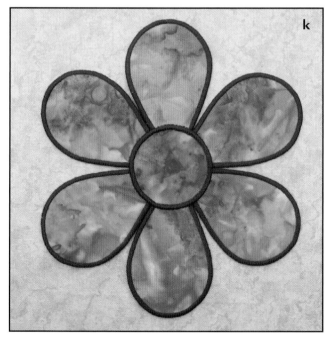

7 Pull the edges of the petals together and join them by machine to the point marked on the template (**l**). Your first bowl is now finished!

Other tricks and tips

- The example I used above shows you how to assemble one of the basic bowl designs that's made up like a flower. Some of the other patterns in the book – for instance the Green Leaves (page 44), the Duck-Pond (page 82), Teddies (page 81) and Gingerbread Men (page 26) – use shaped patches which you stitch around completely (**a**) before you add them to the base (**b**) and then join them.

- On most of the templates, you'll find arrows which give you important information about joining the bowl sides. On designs such as the basic flowers, for instance the Primrose, you'll pull the sides up and join them to the point marked on the template (**c** and **d**).

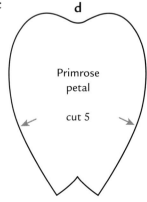

Primrose petal

cut 5

Assembling the bowls

On other designs, the arrows indicate the parts of the shapes that will butt up against each other and be joined – for instance on the Bright Easter Eggs bowl (**e** and **f**).

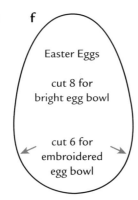

e **f**

Easter Eggs

cut 8 for bright egg bowl

cut 6 for embroidered egg bowl

- When you come to stitching up the sides of each design to form a bowl shape, you have two choices: to stitch by hand or by machine. Almost all of these bowl designs can be joined by machine, which is much quicker, and also stronger. I use a medium-width and medium-length zigzag (about 2 and 2), stitching in the same thread that I've used to edge the patches; if you use this technique, you'll find that the joining stitches blend in with the satin stitch edgings.

There are a few designs in the book where the sides can only be joined by hand, as the angle between the base and the sides is too steep to get under the machine comfortably. When you're stitching these joins, use a double thread (for strength) and join the edges with ladder stitch to create a strong, invisible join. You'll also find this technique useful for times when you need to join two patches which are edged in different colours of thread – for instance the Duck-Pond on page 82, and the Rainbow Hexagon on page 80. When the edge patches of a bowl overlap, for instance the Poppy (page 68) and Briar Rose (page 67), work on the outside of the bowl and use a slipstitch to attach the overlapping layer to the underneath one invisibly.

- Occasionally through the book I've joined the bowl sides in different ways rather than stitching them. For instance on the Tulips (page 60) I've stitched a bead in between each flower tip; on the Fans (page 52) I've also used beads as decoration on the overlapping corners. For the Braided Bowl on page 89 I've pulled up the sides with a circle of braid, then stitched the braid in place on each patch. You could try these techniques on some of the other bowl designs, too, instead of joining them conventionally.

Stitching

The satin stitch that you work around the bowl patches is the key to your bowl's success, so it's well worth while spending the time getting your stitch just right. You're aiming to produce an attractive, even satin stitch with good coverage of your fabric. If you haven't come across the idea of a machine satin stitch before, it's essentially just a very close zigzag; the stitches are worked so close together that they create a virtually solid band of stitching.

1 First of all, check which foot you need on your machine to allow you to do zigzag, and fix it on. If you have an open-toed appliqué foot, or a clear appliqué foot, put this on instead of an ordinary zigzag foot; you'll find that it really helps you to see where you're going.

2 Now identify the knob/button/switch that controls the stitch length on your machine. (You'll be surprised how many people aren't quite sure where this is on their machine!) If you haven't played around with this control before, put a doubled piece of scrap fabric under the machine foot and try increasing and decreasing the stitch length, stitching for an inch or two each time until you feel comfortable with altering the stitch.

3 Next, identify the control for your stitch width. Once again, play around with this until you're familiar with its effects.

4 Now you're ready to set your machine up to satin stitch. Set the stitch *width* to about 3.5 or 4; machines vary enormously in how the actual stitch comes out, but I find on my Bernina that 4 is the ideal width for the satin stitch on most of these bowl designs. Set the stitch *length* to about 1, and put a fresh piece of folded scrap fabric under your machine foot. Your aim now is to see how small you can make your stitch length to produce a good, close satin stitch while still allowing the fabric to feed smoothly under the machine foot. Start stitching, and gradually reduce the stitch length till you have a nice close stitch. Remember that you'll be going over the edge of each patch twice (see page 7), so don't worry if you still have fractional gaps between the stitches.

5 Once you're happy with your stitch, work two rows of satin stitch round the edge of each patch as instructed. Your aim is to get the right-hand edge of the satin stitch going just over the right-hand edge of the patch (right), so that the stitching seals the raw edge.

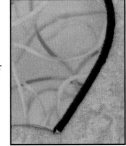

Tips for good satin stitch

- When your machine is doing satin stitch, it moves the fabric very slowly under the foot as the stitches are so close together. To help you keep the satin stitch smooth, resist the temptation to pull the fabric through faster!

- If you have a Bernina, look on the little arm of the bobbin case; at the end of the arm you'll see a tiny hole. When you're setting up your machine for satin stitch, put the bobbin in the case and then put the thread through that little hole; this will help to produce a really good smooth stitch.

- When you've cut the patches for your bowl out of the fabric-covered interfacing, keep some of the offcuts of interfacing. When you're ready to start stitching, try your stitch out on the offcuts first; this will help you to select just the right stitch width and length – and will also show you how well your chosen thread works on the fabric.

- Even with the smartest machines, you'll find that the upper side of the satin stitch looks smoother than the underside. Use this smoother side as the inside of the bowl, as the inside will be on view more than the outside.

- If you're working spirals on your design (for instance on the Oriental Clouds on page 53 or the Nautilus Shells on page 36), practise the spirals on scrap pieces of covered interfacing first, till you're confident of creating them smoothly. If you find it too tricky to taper the stitching towards the centre of your spirals, just keep the stitch width the same and finish the spiral off securely in the middle.

- If you find it difficult to stitch points neatly (for instance on the blackwork bowl on page 14), this is where the felt pens come into their own! Choose a permanent felt pen or fabric marking pen in a colour that matches your satin stitching, and dab the point carefully onto any areas of interfacing that are showing through slightly. If you're still not quite happy, or your stitching is a bit chunky on the points, stitch on a bead; it's a great way of neatening things up.

Embellishing

Once you've mastered assembling a basic bowl, you'll think of all kinds of ways in which you can embellish your designs. Try some of these:

- Add beads, buttons or charms. I've used this idea on things like the Mushrooms (page 45) and the Gingerbread Men (page 26); you'll find it easiest to stitch a bead on both sides of the shape at the same time, taking the needle through to each side in turn. Once both beads (or buttons etc) are stitched firmly in place, finish off the thread securely.

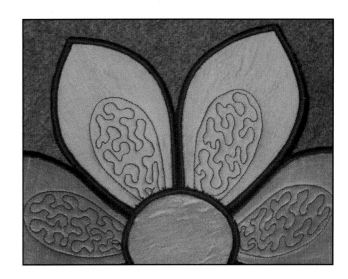

- Decorate the patches with sew-on jewels.
- Add machine quilting – as I've done on the bases for several bowls such as the Starfish (page 37).
- Embroider designs or lines on the patches. I used variations of this idea on the Butterflies (page 54), the Starfish (page 37) and the Briar Rose (page 67).
- Embellish the covered strip of interfacing with random lines of machine embroidery/quilting; I've done this with the fabric I used for the Easter Basket (page 32).
- Work vermicelli/stipple quilting across the covered interfacing, or free machining in different patterns (see above, and the Blazing Sun bowl on page 87).

Making a blackwork bowl

On several bowls in the book I've used fancy stitches on my machine to embellish the covered interfacing before I cut out the petals. The Embroidered Eggs on page 31 make use of this technique, and all the bowls in the Jacobean Jewels collection (see pages 58-62) use variations, working in black so that the embroidery creates the effect of traditional blackwork.

If you'd like to try a simple bowl embellished in this way, cut a strip of interfacing 20 x 5in (51 x 12.5cm) and fuse a strip of fabric to each side: then use a long quilt rule and a chalk marker to mark lines at 1in intervals across the strip. Work automatic machine stitches in black down these lines and at random intervals between the lines (I think the stitching looks prettiest if the intervals aren't too even); use a variety of different stitches, some open and some more solid, for visual interest (**a**).

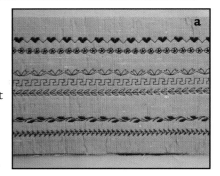

Using either of the blackwork petal templates on page 95, mark your petals (**b**) and cut them out (**c**), then edge the petals in black (**d**) and construct the bowl in the usual way (**e**). If you like, you can decorate the centre circle with stitching too, before you assemble the bowl (**f** and **g**).

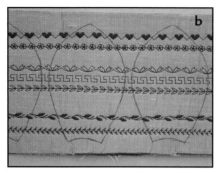

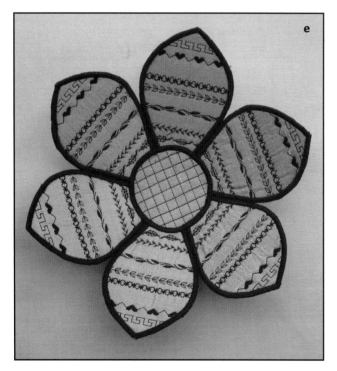

Over to you ...

If you're already familiar with my work, you'll know that I love it when people take my basic ideas and take them on further, adding their own ideas and inspiration. You'll think of lots of ways of adding your own touch to my designs, and that's just the way I like it. One way you can easily vary the designs is by enlarging or reducing them; because there are no seam allowances to worry about, doing this is ridiculously simple: just photocopy (or scan) all the templates for a particular bowl, then enlarge or reduce them by the same percentage. Then you're ready to go! Remember, though, that the materials requirements will vary according to the new size of your design.

Another way in which can vary the designs is by using more side shapes round a larger base: this is what I've done with the two easter egg designs on pages 30 and 31, using six egg patches round one circular base and eight eggs round a larger one. Try the shapes out in paper first of all to check how the shapes and sizes work together.

If you're inspired to create your own bowl designs, work in stiff paper first so that you can see how the shapes work together and adapt them till they're just right. I tape them together with little strips of sticky tape so that I can see how they behave round the bases and when the sides are drawn up. Once you're satisfied that the patches all work together, then you can cut them from the covered interfacing. And if you create any bowls you're particularly pleased with, I'd love to see a photograph! My contact details are on page 96.

Assembling the bowls

The Flower Garden

Flowers are some of the best inspirations you can get for quilted bowls – they come in such a breathtaking variety of shapes, colours, sizes and textures. For this collection I've chosen just a few shapes from the extravaganza you'll find in any flower-filled garden – but don't forget that you can vary these to represent lots of other flowers, too.

Marigold

Vivid orange marigolds create bright spots wherever they grow; capture their bold good looks in a simple bowl. This is a versatile shape that you can easily use to create other flowers; make a Michaelmas daisy using blue or purple petals and a green-yellow centre, a traditional daisy with white petals round a yellow centre, or a bright pink-petalled gerbera.

Difficulty rating ✪

Materials

***Option A**, if you're making the petals from just two fabrics, as I've done:*

* fusible interfacing:
  for the petals, one 20 x 4½in (51 x 11.5cm) strip
  for the centre, one 3in (7.5cm) square

* fabrics:
  for the petals, strips of two different orange fabrics, each 20 x 4½in (51 x 11.5cm)
  for the centre, two 3in (7.5cm) squares of orangey-brown

***Option B**, if you're making each petal in a different fabric:*

* fusible interfacing:
  for the petals, eight 2½ x 4½in (6.5 x 11.5cm) patches
  for the centre, one 3in (7.5cm) square

* fabrics:
  for the petals, sixteen 2½ x 4½in (6.5 x 11.5cm) patches, two of each fabric
  for the centre, two 3in (7.5cm) squares of orangey-brown

You will also need:

* Black sewing thread

Instructions

1 **Option A** Prepare the strip of interfacing by fusing one orange fabric on one side, and the second on the other side. Use the appropriate template on page 20 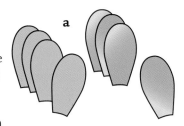 to mark eight petals and cut them out in the usual way, but remember to use four of the petals up one way when you stitch them, and four up the other way so that the second fabric shows on the top (**a**).

Option B Fuse the fabrics onto the individual patches of interfacing in matching pairs, then use the template on page 20 to mark one petal shape on each prepared patch. Cut out the petals.

2 Prepare the patch for the flower centre, then use template A on page 92 to mark the centre circle; cut out the shape (**b**).

3 Work two layers of satin stitch around the curved edges of the petals (**c**); don't stitch across the bottom edge of the petal shapes.

4 Lay the centre circle on a flat surface and arrange the petals evenly around it (**d**); the petals should just touch each other, and will tuck slightly under the edges of the centre circle. Pin firmly in place.

5 Work two circuits of zigzag round the edge of the centre circle to secure the petals, then trim the bottoms of the petals on the back of the work if necessary. Work two circuits of satin stitch round the edges of the centre circle (**e**).

6 Pull the edges of the petals together and join them by machine to the point marked on the template. If you prefer a slightly flatter bowl you could make the lines of stitching a bit shorter, but don't join the edges further up than the marked point, otherwise the petals will start to pull out of shape.

TIP I used two different orange prints for this flower, but it would look equally good in a marbled or batik orange fabric.

Periwinkle

The wonderfully-named periwinkle, or vinca, comes in two sizes: vinca major and vinca minor (sound like two brothers at a public school ...). Now, here's a third size: vinca giganta! I've taken the asymmetric petal shapes of the periwinkle and made them into a bowl, arranging the petals around a small central pentagon.

Difficulty rating ✪

Materials

Option A, if you're making all the petals from the same fabric, as I've done:

- fusible interfacing:
  for the petals, one 19 x 5in (48 x 13cm) strip
  for the centre, one 3in (7.5cm) square

- fabrics:
  for the petals, two 19 x 5in (48 x 13cm) strips of blue
  for the centre, two 3in (7.5cm) squares of pale green

Option B, if you're making each petal in a different fabric:

- fusible interfacing:
  for the petals, five 4 x 5in (10 x 13cm) patches
  for the centre, one 3in (7.5cm) square

- fabrics:
  ten 4 x 5in (10 x 13cm) patches, two of each fabric
  for the centre, two 3in (7.5cm) squares of pale green

You will also need:

- Black sewing thread

Instructions

1 **Option A** Prepare the strip of inter-facing by fusing the strips of blue fabric onto it. Use the appropriate template on page 20 to mark five petals, and cut them out in the usual way (**a**).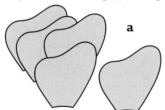

   Option B Fuse the fabrics onto the individual patches of interfacing in matching pairs, then use the template on page 20 to mark one petal shape on each prepared patch. Cut out the petals.

2 Prepare the patch for the flower centre, then use the curved pentagon on page 20 to mark the centre shape and cut it out (**b**).

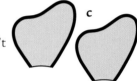

3 Work two layers of satin stitch around the curved edges of the petals (**c**); don't stitch across the bottom edge of the petal shapes.

4 Lay the centre pentagon on a flat surface and arrange the petals evenly around it (**d**); the petals should just touch each other, and will tuck slightly under the edges of the centre circle. Pin firmly in place.

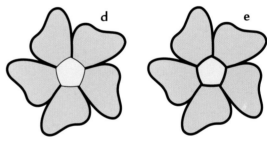

5 Work two circuits of zigzag round the edge of the centre pentagon to secure the petals, then trim the bottoms of the petals on the back of the work if necessary. Work two lines of satin stitch round the edges of the centre shape (**e**).

6 Pull the edges of the petals together and join them by machine to the point marked on the template.

TIP I used a slightly mottled blue fabric for the petals; a batik or hand-dyed blue would look nice too – or try an allover print for a more zany, abstract flower.

Black-Eyed Susan

The bright yellow petals of this daisy-like flower are made even more dramatic with their black framing, and simple lines of machine quilting add a realistic texture to the petals. This is another design that's easily adapted to create other flowers — and it would work well in a bright jazzy print, too, or a soft pastel batik.

Difficulty rating ✪ ✪

Materials

***Option A**, if you're making all the petals from the same fabric, as I've done:*

- fusible interfacing:
  for the petals, one 16 x 5in (41 x 13cm) strip
  for the centre, one 3in (7.5cm) square

- fabrics:
  for the petals, two 16 x 5in (41 x 13cm) strips of yellow
  for the centre, two 3in (7.5cm) squares of black or dark brown

***Option B**, if you're making each petal in a different fabric:*

- fusible interfacing:
  for the petals, eight 2½ x 5in (6.5 x 13cm) patches
  for the centre, one 3in (7.5cm) square

- fabrics:
  for the petals, sixteen 2½ x 5in (6.5 x 13cm) patches, two of each fabric
  for the centre, two 3in (7.5cm) squares of black or dark brown

You will also need:

- Black and yellow sewing threads

Instructions

1 **Option A** Prepare the strip of interfacing by fusing the strips of yellow fabric onto it. Use the appropriate template on page 20 to mark eight petals, and cut them out in the usual way (**a**).

   Option B Fuse the fabrics onto the individual patches of interfacing in matching pairs, then use the template on page 20 to mark one petal shape on each prepared patch. Cut out the petals.

2 Prepare the patch for the flower centre, then use template A on page 92 to mark the centre circle; cut out the shape (**b**).

3 Working in yellow thread, stitch four or five random lines of straight stitch down the length of each petal (**c**).

4 Work two layers of black satin stitch around the curved edges of the petals (**d**), making a nice sharp point at the top; don't stitch across the bottom edge of the petal shapes.

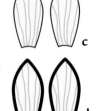

5 Lay the centre circle on a flat surface and arrange the petals evenly around it (**e**); the petals should just touch each other, and will tuck slightly under the edges of the centre circle. Pin firmly in place.

6 Work two circuits of zigzag round the edge of the centre circle to secure the petals, then trim the bottoms of the petals on the back of the work if necessary. Work two lines of satin stitch round the edges of the centre circle (**f**).

7 Pull the edges of the petals together and join them by machine to the point marked on the template. If you prefer a slightly flatter bowl you could make the lines of stitching a bit shorter, but don't join the edges further up than the marked point, otherwise the petals will start to distort.

TIP Try not to make the quilting lines on the petals too symmetrical, so that the flower looks nice and natural.

Primula

The primula is the tame version of the wild primrose, and is found in a much wider range of colours – particularly deep bluey purples, crimsons and pinks, as well as bright yellows and oranges. If you want to make a series of bowls with a unifying theme, you could make a whole mantelpiece-full just using this pattern in different colours!

Difficulty rating ✿

Materials

Option A, if you're making all the petals from the same fabric, as I've done:

- fusible interfacing:
   for the petals, one 18 x 4½in (46 x 11.5cm) strip
   for the centre, one 3in (7.5cm) square

- fabrics:
   for the petals, two 18 x 4½in (46 x 11.5cm) strips of purple
   for the centre, two 3in (7.5cm) squares of yellow

Option B, if you're making each petal in a different fabric:

- fusible interfacing:
   for the petals, five 4 x 4½in (10 x 11.5cm) patches
   for the centre, one 3in (7.5cm) square

- fabrics:
   for the petals, ten 4 x 4½in (10 x 11.5cm) patches, two of each fabric
   for the centre, two 3in (7.5cm) squares of yellow

You will also need:

- Black sewing thread

Instructions

1 **Option A** Prepare the strip of interfacing by fusing the strips of purple fabric onto it. Use the appropriate template on page 20 to mark five petals, and cut them out in the usual way (**a**).

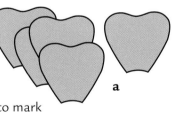

Option B Fuse the fabrics onto the individual patches of interfacing in matching pairs, then use the appropriate template on page 20 to mark one petal shape on each prepared patch. Cut out the petals.

2 Prepare the patch for the flower centre, then use template A on page 92 to mark the centre circle and cut it out (**b**).

3 Work two layers of satin stitch around the curved edges of the petals (**c**); don't stitch across the bottom edge of the petal shapes.

4 Lay the centre circle on a flat surface and arrange the petals evenly around it (**d**); the petals should just touch each other, and will tuck slightly under the edges of the centre circle. Pin firmly in place.

5 Work two circuits of zigzag round the edge of the centre circle to secure the petals, then trim the bottoms of the petals on the back of the work if necessary. Work two lines of satin stitch round the edges of the centre shape (**e**).

6 Pull the edges of the petals together and join them by machine to the point marked on the template.

TIP The random-dyed fabric I chose for this flower creates more visual interest on the petals than a flat, plain colour.

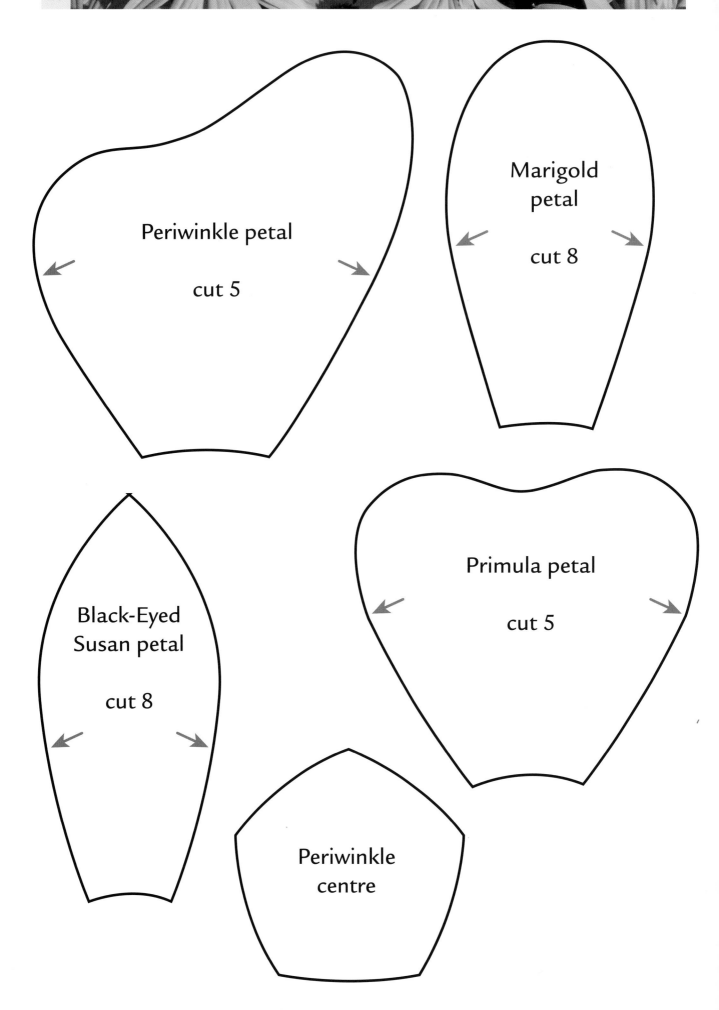

Periwinkle petal

cut 5

Marigold
petal

cut 8

Black-Eyed
Susan petal

cut 8

Primula petal

cut 5

Periwinkle
centre

The Flower Garden: *Templates*

Christmas Treats

At Christmas-time, there's always a deluge of attractive sweets and snacks – chocolates, nuts, clementines, foil-wrapped sweets, candy sticks. Show them off in a collection of seasonal bowls created in Christmassy prints. You can also use these bowls to display baubles and other trinkets, or pine-cones and walnuts sprayed gold or silver.

Midnight Stars

Metallic print fabrics look lovely in Christmas projects, and I've used two for this design – the star-shaped side sections are in midnight blue marbled with gold, and the base is a deep rich red printed with gold star motifs. By using a tan rayon thread, I've created the effect of a golden-coloured outline without having to deal with metallic threads.

Difficulty rating ✪ ✪

Materials

Option A, *if you're making all the petals from the same fabric, as I've done:*

- fusible interfacing:
  for the stars, one 26 x 6in (66 x 15cm) strip
  for the base, one 6½in (16.5cm) square

- fabrics:
  for the stars, two 26 x 6in (66 x 15cm) strips
  for the base, two 6½in (16.5cm) squares

Option B, *if you're making each star in a different fabric:*

- fusible interfacing:
  for the stars, five 6in (15cm) squares
  for the base, one 6½in (16.5cm) square

- fabrics:
  for the stars, ten 6in (15cm) squares, two of each colour
  for the base, two 6½in (16.5cm) squares

You will also need:

- Contrasting sewing thread

Instructions

1 **Option A** Prepare the strip of interfacing by fusing the strips of fabric onto it. Use the template on page 27 to mark five star shapes, and cut them out in the usual way (**a**).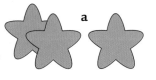

   Option B Fuse the fabrics onto the individual patches of interfacing in matching pairs, then use the template on page 27 to mark one star shape on each prepared patch. Cut out the stars.

2 Work two layers of satin stitch all around the edge of each star shape (**b**).

3 Prepare the patch for the base, then use pentagon template J on page 94 to mark the centre shape and cut it out (**c**). Trim each corner very slightly to create a small curve (**d**),

then work two layers of satin stitch around the edge of the shape (**e**).

4 Lay the base shape on a flat surface, then arrange the star shapes around it, one on each side of the pentagon (**f**); pin firmly in place where the stars touch the edge of the base.

5 Use a few strong hand or machine stitches to secure the stars to the base where they touch; don't stitch for more than about ¼in (6mm), otherwise the stars will pull out of shape.

6 Pull the edges of the stars together so that the lower arms of the stars touch just above the base; join by hand or machine as before. Now do the same with the upper arms of the stars to complete the bowl.

TIP For a smaller version of the same design, use a photocopier to reduce both templates to 90% or 85%.

Poinsettia

I don't have much success in keeping poinsettias alive; even if I buy one just before Christmas I often can't even keep it going till the day itself! Finally I've solved the problem: create my own permanent poinsettia bloom, which I can bring out year after year … (And incidentally, I know that strictly they're bracts, but petals is a prettier word!)

Difficulty rating ✪ ✪

Materials

Option A, *if you're making all the petals from the same fabric:*

- fusible interfacing:
  for the petals, one 24 x 6in (61 x 15cm) strip
  for the centre, one 3in (7.5cm) square

- fabrics:
  for the petals, two 24 x 6in (61 x 15cm) strips of red
  for the centre, two 3in (7.5cm) squares of yellow

Option B, *if you're making each petal in a different fabric:*

- fusible interfacing:
  for the petals, nine 3 x 6in (7.5 x 15cm) patches
  for the centre, one 3in (7.5cm) square

- fabrics:
  for the petals, eighteen 3 x 6in (7.5 x 15cm) patches of red, two of each fabric
  for the centre, two 3in (7.5cm) squares of yellow

You will also need:

- Black sewing thread
- Chalk marker

Instructions

1 **Option A** Prepare the strip of interfacing by fusing the strips of red fabric onto it. Use the template on page 28 to mark nine petal shapes, and cut them out in the usual way (**a**).

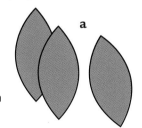

Option B Fuse the fabrics onto the individual patches of interfacing in matching pairs, then use the template on page 28 to mark one petal shape on each prepared patch. Cut out the petals.

2 Beginning at one point, work two layers of satin stitch all around the edge of each petal shape (**b**).

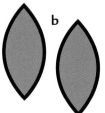

3 Prepare the patch for the centre, then use the circular template A on page 92 to mark the central circle and cut it out (**c**). Work two layers of satin stitch all around the circle (**d**).

4 Lay the centre patch on a flat surface and position the petals evenly around it (**e**); pin firmly in place.

5 Use just a few strong machine stitches to secure each petal where it touches the edge of the base.

6 On each petal, make dots of chalk at the points marked on the template. Pull the edges of the petals together so that they just touch, and join them by machine between the dots to create the bowl shape.

TIP If you fancy making your petals in three alternating fabrics, as I've done, cut three 9 x 6in (23 x 15cm) patches of interfacing and cover each one with a different fabric. Then cut three petal shapes from each prepared patch, stitch them in the usual way, and arrange them in sequence around the yellow centre.

The Heart of Christmas

Use a variety of folksy Christmas prints to create the heart shapes for this bowl; quilt shops often sell collections of toning prints which are ideal for this kind of project. I've added simple heart buttons to decorate the side pieces, stitching the pairs of buttons in a different place on each heart.

Difficulty rating ✪ ✪

Materials

Option A, *if you're making all the hearts from the same fabric:*

- fusible interfacing:
  for the hearts, one 24 x 4½in (46 x 11.5cm) strip
  for the base, one 4½in (11.5cm) square

- fabrics:
  for the hearts, two 24 x 4½in (46 x 11.5cm) strips
  for the base, two 4½in (11.5cm) squares

Option B, *if you're making each heart in a different fabric, as I've done:*

- fusible interfacing:
  for the hearts, six 4 x 4½in (10 x 11.5cm) patches
  for the base, one 4½in (11.5cm) square

- fabric:
  for the hearts, twelve 4 x 4½in (10 x 11.5cm) patches, two of each colour
  for the base, two 4½in (11.5cm) squares

You will also need:

- Contrasting sewing thread
- Chalk marker
- Twelve heart buttons or charms and matching thread

Instructions

1 **Option A** Prepare the strip of interfacing by fusing the strips of fabric onto it. Use the template on page 27 to mark six heart shapes, alternating the direction each time so that the hearts fit in (**a**), and cut them out in the usual way (**b**).

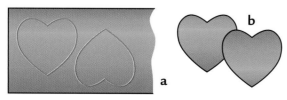

Option B If you're using any directional prints or stripes, make sure that you've cut the patches in the

right direction across the fabric. Fuse the fabrics onto the individual patches of interfacing in matching pairs, then use the template on page 27 to mark one heart shape on each prepared patch. Cut out the hearts.

2 Beginning at the tip, work two layers of satin stitch all around the edge of each heart shape (**c**).

3 Stitch the heart buttons or charms onto the heart shapes (**d**), stitching them in pairs through each shape.

4 Prepare the patch for the centre, then use the circular template D on page 92 to mark the central circle and cut it out (**e**). Work two layers of satin stitch all around the circle (**f**).

5 Lay the centre circle on a flat surface and position the hearts evenly around it (**g**); pin firmly in place.

6 Use just a few strong machine stitches to secure the tip of each heart where it touches the edge of the base.

7 On each heart, make dots of chalk at the points marked on the template. Pull the edges of the hearts together so that they just touch, and join them by machine between the dots to create the bowl shape.

TIP Don't worry if you have a few slightly loose or uneven stitches at the bottom of the hearts; these will be hidden by the stitching that secures the shapes to the base.

Doves of Peace

To give these doves an ethereal appearance I've cut the shapes from a beautiful frosted fabric in shades of blue and silver, and edged them with blue. The design would look equally good, though, in shades of yellow and gold, or in Christmas folk-prints stitched with black or dark red thread.

Difficulty rating ✪ ✪ ✪

Materials

***Option A**, if you're making all the doves from the same fabric, as I've done:*

- fusible interfacing:
  for the doves, one 19 x 6in (48 x 15cm) strip
  for the centre, one 6½in (16.5cm) square

- fabrics:
  for the doves, two 19 x 6in (48 x 15cm) strips
  for the centre, two 6½in (16.5cm) squares

***Option B**, if you're making each dove in a different fabric:*

- fusible interfacing:
  for the doves, five 4½ x 6in (11.5 x 15cm) patches
  for the centre, one 6½in (16.5cm) square

- fabrics:
  for the doves, ten 4½ x 6in (11.5 x 15cm) patches, two of each colour
  for the centre, two 6½in (16.5cm) squares

You will also need:

- Contrasting sewing thread
- Ten small round beads for the eyes

Instructions

1 **Option A** Prepare the strip of interfacing by fusing the strips of fabric onto it. Use the template on page 28 to mark five dove shapes, and cut them out in the usual way (**a**).

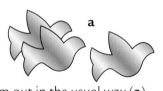

Option B Fuse the fabrics onto the individual patches of interfacing in matching pairs, then use the template on page 28 to mark one dove shape on each prepared patch. Cut out the doves.

2 Prepare the patch for the bowl base, then use pentagon template J on page 94 to mark the centre shape and cut it out (**b**). Work two layers of satin stitch around the pentagon (**c**).

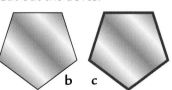

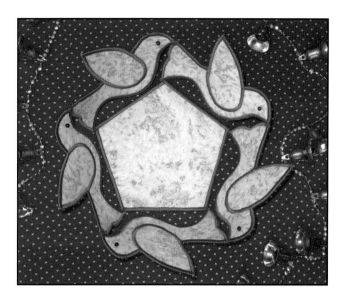

3 Beginning at the point where the head shape goes into the wing, work two layers of satin stitch around the outlines of the dove shapes (**d**). Next, work two layers of satin stitch around the wing (**e**). Don't begin at the tip of the wing, as this is quite a sharp point and it can be difficult to finish off the stitching line neatly; instead, begin near one end of your previous stitching line.

4 Stitch a little bead to each side of each dove to form the eyes (**f**), stitching them in pairs through the dove shapes; the template shows where the beads should go.

5 Lay the centre shape on a flat surface and position the doves around it as shown (**g**); pin firmly in place. Use a few strong machine stitches to join the tip of each dove's tail to one corner of the pentagon.

6 Pull the dove shapes up and pin them so that each dove's beak touches the top tail tip of the one in front; join them with a few strong stitches by hand or machine.

TIP If you prefer a less open bowl, join the doves to the centre at the tail tip and the tummy; then overlap the dove shapes a little and slipstitch them together by hand on the outside of the bowl.

Gingerbread Men

Novelty gingerbread shapes decorated with white icing and coloured sweets – for many years these have been traditional Christmas treats in Scandinavia and central Europe. Instead of the consumable versions, make these cheerful stitched alternatives and they'll last a little bit longer!

Difficulty rating ✿ ✿ ✿ ✿

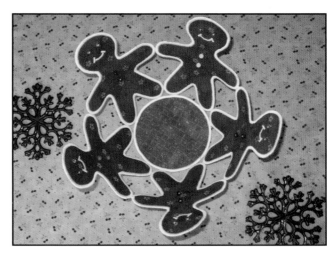

Materials

Option A, *if you're making all the gingerbread men from the same fabric, as I've done:*

- fusible interfacing:
  for the gingerbread men, one 26 x 7in (66 x 18cm) strip
  for the base, one 5in (13cm) square

- fabrics:
  for the gingerbread men, two 26 x 7in (66 x 18cm) strips
  for the base, two 5in (13cm) squares

Option B, *if you're making each gingerbread man in a different fabric:*

- fusible interfacing:
  for the gingerbread men, five 5½ x 7in (14 x 18cm) patches
  for the base, one 5in (13cm) square

- fabrics:
  for the gingerbread men, ten 5½ x 7in (14 x 18cm) patches, two of each colour
  for the base, two 5in (13cm) squares

You will also need:

- White sewing thread
- 20 small round beads for the eyes, 20 medium round beads for the buttons (four of each colour), and matching sewing threads

Instructions

1 **Option A** Prepare the strip of interfacing by fusing the strips of fabric onto it. Use the template on page 28 to mark five gingerbread man shapes, and cut them out in the usual way (**a**).

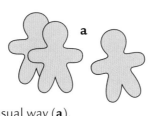

Option B Fuse the fabrics onto the individual patches of interfacing in matching pairs, then use the template on page 28 to mark one gingerbread man shape on each prepared patch. Cut out the shapes.

2 Prepare the patch for the base, then use circle template E on page 92 to mark the centre circle and cut it out (**b**).

3 Work two layers of satin stitch all around the edges of each gingerbread man (**c**); begin at the crotch – this will make the beginning and the end of your stitching less noticeable.

4 Follow the markings on the template to stitch a smile on each man, using a narrow satin stitch. Stitch on the eyes, then add the buttons to each shape (**d**), stitching all the beads and buttons on in pairs through the shape. It's much easier to embellish the shapes before you join them to the base – that way, you only have to work on a small, flat patch.

5 Work two layers of satin stitch all around the edges of the base (**e**). Lay the base on a flat surface and arrange the gingerbread men evenly around it (**f**), so that the bottoms of their legs just touch the edge. Pin firmly in place.

6 Use a few strong hand or machine stitches to secure the ends of the legs to the base where they touch; don't stitch for more than about ¼in (6mm), otherwise the shapes will distort.

7 Pull the sides up into a bowl shape and use the same method to join the legs of the ginger-bread men where they touch, just above the base. Once you've stitched all the joins between the legs, pin the arms together so that they just touch and join in the same way.

TIP If you'd like to make some of your shapes into gingerbread women, adapt the basic template as shown and add a little white lace apron to each patch!

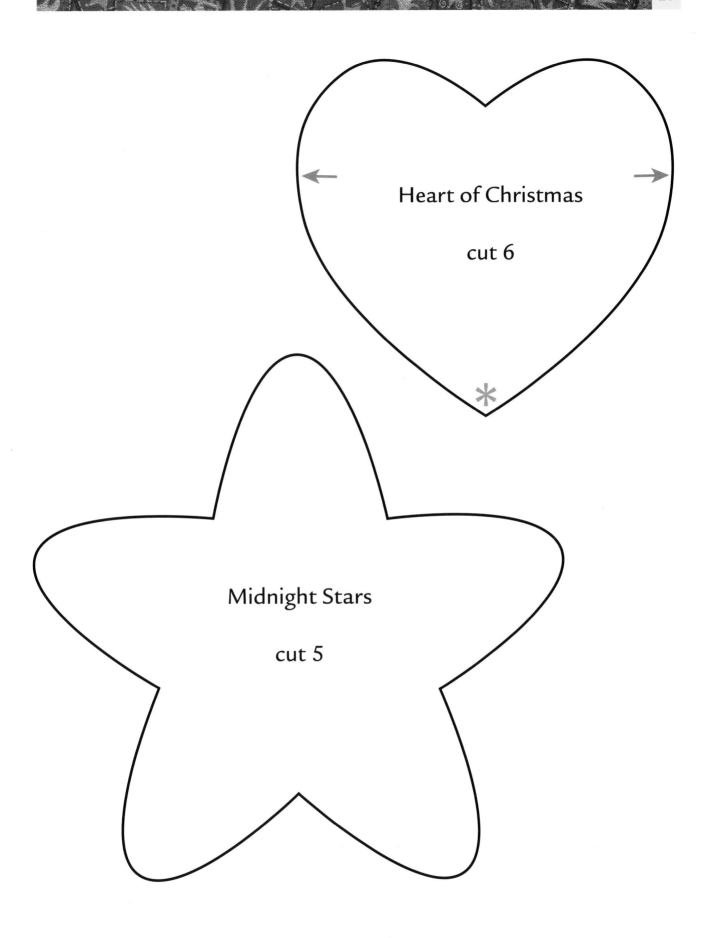

Heart of Christmas

cut 6

Midnight Stars

cut 5

Christmas Treats: *Templates*

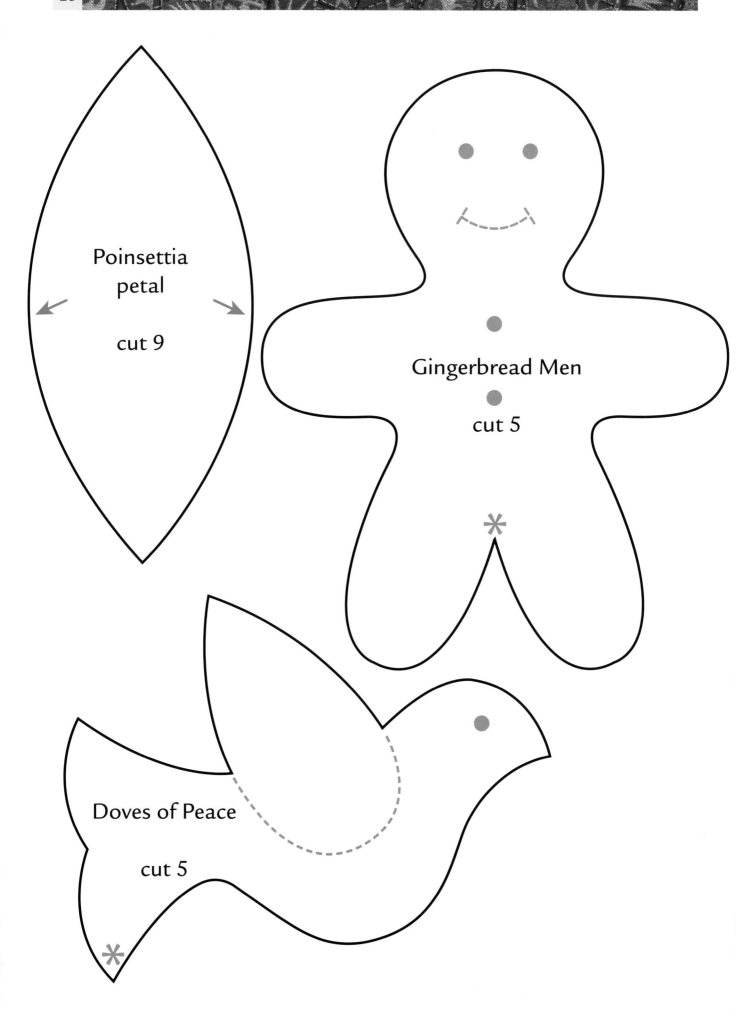

Poinsettia
petal

cut 9

Gingerbread Men

cut 5

Doves of Peace

cut 5

Easter Eggs Etcetera

Foil-wrapped eggs and colourful Easter biscuits are just asking to be shown off in a gorgeous bowl – or why not create a basket, by adding a simple handle to a flower shape? Choose pretty print fabrics in mid-pastel colours, or create your own fancy fabrics by embroidering them with machine stitching.

Bright Easter Eggs

*Use scraps of cheerful print fabrics for this circle of eggs;
the simple shapes let the fabrics speak for themselves – and
make this a very quick bowl to stitch, too! I chose toning
fabrics in shades of blue, purple and mauve, but lots of
other colour-schemes would work well: try spring-like
greens and yellows, or pinks and golds.*

Difficulty rating ✪

Materials

Option A, if you're making all the eggs from the same fabric:

- fusible interfacing:
  for the eggs, one 24 x 4in (61 x 10cm) strip
  for the centre, one 5½in (14cm) square

- fabrics:
  for the eggs, two 24 x 4in (61 x 10cm) strips
  for the centre, two 5½in (14cm) squares

*Option B, if you're using lots of different fabrics for the eggs,
as I've done:*

- fusible interfacing:
  for the eggs, eight 4 x 3in (10 x 7.5cm) patches
  for the centre, one 5½in (14cm) square

- fabrics:
  for the eggs, sixteen 4 x 3in (10 x 7.5cm) patches,
  two of each colour
  for the centre, two 5½in (14cm) squares

You will also need:

- Contrasting sewing thread

Instructions

1 **Option A** Prepare the strip
of interfacing by fusing the
strips of fabric onto it. Use
the egg template on page
34 to mark eight egg
shapes, and cut them out
in the usual way (**a**).

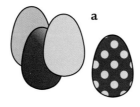

Option B Fuse the fabrics onto the individual
patches of interfacing in matching pairs, then use
the egg template on page 34 to mark one egg shape
on each prepared patch. Cut out the shapes.

2 Prepare the patch for the bowl
base, then use centre template F
on page 93 to mark the circle and
cut it out (**b**).

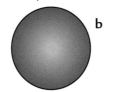

3 Beginning at
the bottom of
the shape, work
two layers of
satin stitch
around each egg (**c**). Now work two
layers of satin stitch around the central circle (**d**).

4 Lay the circular base
on a flat surface and
arrange the eggs
evenly around it (**e**);
I find it helpful to do
this on a grid such
as a cutting board.
Pin firmly in place.

5 Join the bottom of
each egg to the edge of
the base with a few strong
machine stitches; just stitch for about ⅓in (1cm)
each time, otherwise the egg shapes will distort.

6 Pull the egg shapes up and join them where they
touch, using the same technique.

TIP If you're using lots of different fabrics for the egg
shapes, make sure that you choose a thread that's a
good contrast against all of them.

Embroidered Eggs

This smaller egg bowl uses the same egg template as the one opposite, but stitching only six eggs around a smaller base. I've decorated these eggs with lines of machine stitching in soft colours, which creates a very attractive surface – Fabergé would have been proud of them! You could even add beads or jewels if you want the full opulent effect ...

Difficulty rating ✪ ✪ ✪

Materials

Option A, *if you're making all the eggs from the same fabric, as I've done:*

- fusible interfacing:
  for the eggs, one 18 x 4in (46 x 10cm) strip
  for the centre, one 4in (10cm) square

- fabrics:
  for the eggs, two 18 x 4in (46 x 10cm) strips
  for the centre, two 4in (10cm) squares

Option B, *if you're using a different fabric for each egg:*

- fusible interfacing:
  for the eggs, six 4 x 3in (10 x 7.5cm) patches
  for the centre, one 4in (10cm) square

- fabrics:
  for the eggs, twelve 4 x 3in (10 x 7.5cm) patches, two of each colour
  for the centre, two 4in (10cm) squares

You will also need:

- Sewing threads in a selection of pretty colours
- Chalk marker and quilt rule

Instructions

1 **Option A** Prepare the strip of interfacing by fusing the strips of fabric onto it. Use the chalk marker and the quilt rule to draw a few parallel lines down one side of the strip (**a**) – the exact distances between them aren't important. Work a series of pretty automatic stitches down the length of the strip, varying the colours and the stitches as you go. Begin by stitching down the marked lines, then add some other lines of stitching between and beyond the first lines (**b**). Use the egg template on page 34 to mark six egg shapes, and cut them out in the usual way (**c**).

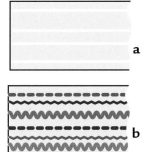

Option B Fuse the fabrics onto the individual patches of interfacing in matching pairs; if you want to add lines of embroidery, do that before you cut out the egg shapes. Use the egg template on page 34 to mark one egg shape on each prepared patch, and cut them out.

2 Prepare the patch for the bowl base, then use centre template C on page 92 to mark the circle and cut it out (**d**).

3 Beginning at the bottom of the shape, work two layers of satin stitch around each egg (**e**). Now work two layers of satin stitch around the central circle (**f**).

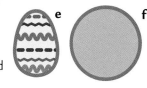

4 Lay the circular base on a flat surface and arrange the eggs evenly around it (**g**); I find it helpful to do this on a grid such as a cutting board. Pin firmly in place.

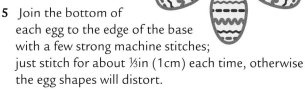

5 Join the bottom of each egg to the edge of the base with a few strong machine stitches; just stitch for about ⅓in (1cm) each time, otherwise the egg shapes will distort.

6 Pull the egg shapes up and join them where they touch, using the same technique.

TIP If you don't have any automatic stitches on your machine, try free quilting the fused strip with the feed dogs down, or cover it with random wiggly lines of stitching as I've done with the Easter Basket design (see page 32).

Easter Basket

A simple flat flower shape is transformed into a basket by the addition of a handle, created from a long strip of interfacing. Use the basket for Easter eggs – or make one for a flower girl to carry at a wedding. I've embellished the petals with random lines of machine quilting, and the handle with a line of decorative stitching.

Difficulty rating ✪ ✪ ✪

Materials

Option A, *if you're making all the petals from the same fabric, as I've done:*

- fusible interfacing:
  for the petals, one 24 x 4in (61 x 10cm) strip
  for the centre, one 4½in (11.5cm) square
  for the handle, one 15 x 1in (38 x 2.5cm) strip

- fabrics:
  for the petals, two 24 x 4in (61 x 10cm) strips
  for the centre, two 4½in (11.5cm) squares
  for the handle, two 15 x 1in (38 x 2.5cm) strips

Option B, *if you're making each petal in a different fabric:*

- fusible interfacing:
  for the petals, eight 3½ x 4in (9 x 10cm) patches
  for the centre, one 4½in (11.5cm) square
  for the handle, one 15 x 1in (38 x 2.5cm) strip

- fabrics:
  for the petals, sixteen 3½ x 4in (9 x 10cm) patches, two of each colour
  for the centre, two 4½in (11.5cm) squares
  for the handle, two 15 x 1in (38 x 2.5cm) strips

You will also need:

- Sewing threads in a selection of bright colours
- Two ribbon roses or flower buttons or charms

Instructions

1 **Option A** Prepare the strip of interfacing by fusing one strip of fabric to each side. Using different colours of thread, work random lines of straight machine stitching across the prepared strip (**a**). Use the easter basket template on page 34 to mark eight petal shapes and cut them out in the usual way (**b**).

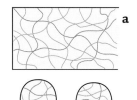

Option B Fuse the fabrics onto the individual patches of interfacing in matching pairs. If you want to embellish the patches, work random lines of machine

stitching across them at this stage, then use the easter basket template on page 34 to mark one petal shape on each prepared patch. Cut out the petals.

2 Prepare the patch for the flower centre, then use centre template D on page 92 to mark the shape; cut it out (**c**).

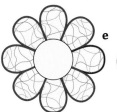

3 Work two layers of satin stitch around the curved edges of the petals (**d**); don't stitch across the bottom edges of the petal shapes.

4 Lay the centre shape on a flat surface and arrange the petals evenly around it (**e**); the petals should just touch each other, and will tuck slightly under the edges of the centre. Pin firmly in place. Work two circuits of zigzag round the edge of the central shape to secure the petals, then trim the bottoms of the petals on the back of the work if necessary. Work two circuits of satin stitch round the edges of the centre (**f**).

5 Pull the edges of the petals together and join them by machine to the point marked on the template. Don't join the edges further up than the marked point, otherwise the petals will start to pull out of shape.

6 Prepare the handle by fusing a strip of fabric onto each side of the interfacing strip. Stitch a line of decorative machine stitching down the centre of the handle, then trim a little off each side of the handle strip so that it's now about ¾in (2cm) wide. Curve the ends of the handle evenly, then work two layers of satin stitch all around the shape (**g**).

7 Pin the handle in place across the basket, then hand-stitch the ends in place; stitch a ribbon rose or flower charm to each end of the handle on the outside of the bowl.

Asymmetric Flower

This wacky flower was inspired by a necklace I saw in a magazine; I loved the idea of a flower with different-sized petals, and realised that it would work well as a bowl. I've made my version from alternating blue and yellow fabrics, but as the flower isn't in any way realistic, all kinds of colour-schemes would work well!

Difficulty rating ✪ ✪ ✪

Materials

- fusible interfacing:

  for petal A, one 3 x 6½in (7.5 x 16.5cm) patch

  for petals B and H, two 3 x 6in (7.5 x 15cm) patches

  for petals C and G, two 3 x 5½in (7.5 x 14cm) patches

  for petals D and F, two 2½ x 4½in (6.5 x 11.5cm) patches

  for petal E, one 2½ x 4in (6.5 x 10cm) patch

  for the centre, one 3in (7.5cm) square

- fabrics:

  for petal A, two 3 x 6½in (7.5 x 16.5cm) patches

  for petals B and H, four 3 x 6in (7.5 x 15cm) patches, two of each fabric

  for petals C and G, four 3 x 5½in (7.5 x 14cm) patches, two of each fabric

  for petals D and F, four 2½ x 4½in (6.5 x 11.5cm) patches, two of each fabric

  for petal E, two 2½ x 4in (6.5 x 10cm) patches

  for the centre, two 3in (7.5cm) squares

You will also need:

- Contrasting sewing thread

Instructions

1 Fuse the fabrics onto the individual patches of interfacing in matching pairs. Use the five pointed petal templates on page 34 to mark the appropriate petal shape onto each prepared patch, and cut them out (**a**).

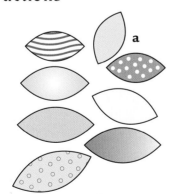

2 Prepare the patch for the bowl base, then use centre template A on page 92 to mark the circle and cut it out (**b**). Work two layers of satin stitch around the central circle (**c**).

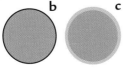

3 Beginning at the bottom point of each petal, work two layers of satin stitch around each shape (**d**).

4 Lay the circular base on a flat surface and arrange the petals in order around it, spacing the points evenly around the circumference (**e**); I find it helpful to do this on a grid such as a cutting board. Pin firmly in place.

5 Join the bottom of each petal to the edge of the base with just a couple of strong machine stitches.

6 Pull the petals up and pin them together to create a good bowl shape; keep adjusting the pins until you can see just where the petals need to join to create the shape you want. When you're happy, use a few strong stitches to join the pairs of petals where they touch.

TIP You could join the petals of this flower with toning beads instead of with stitching.

Easter Eggs Etcetera: Asymmetric Flower

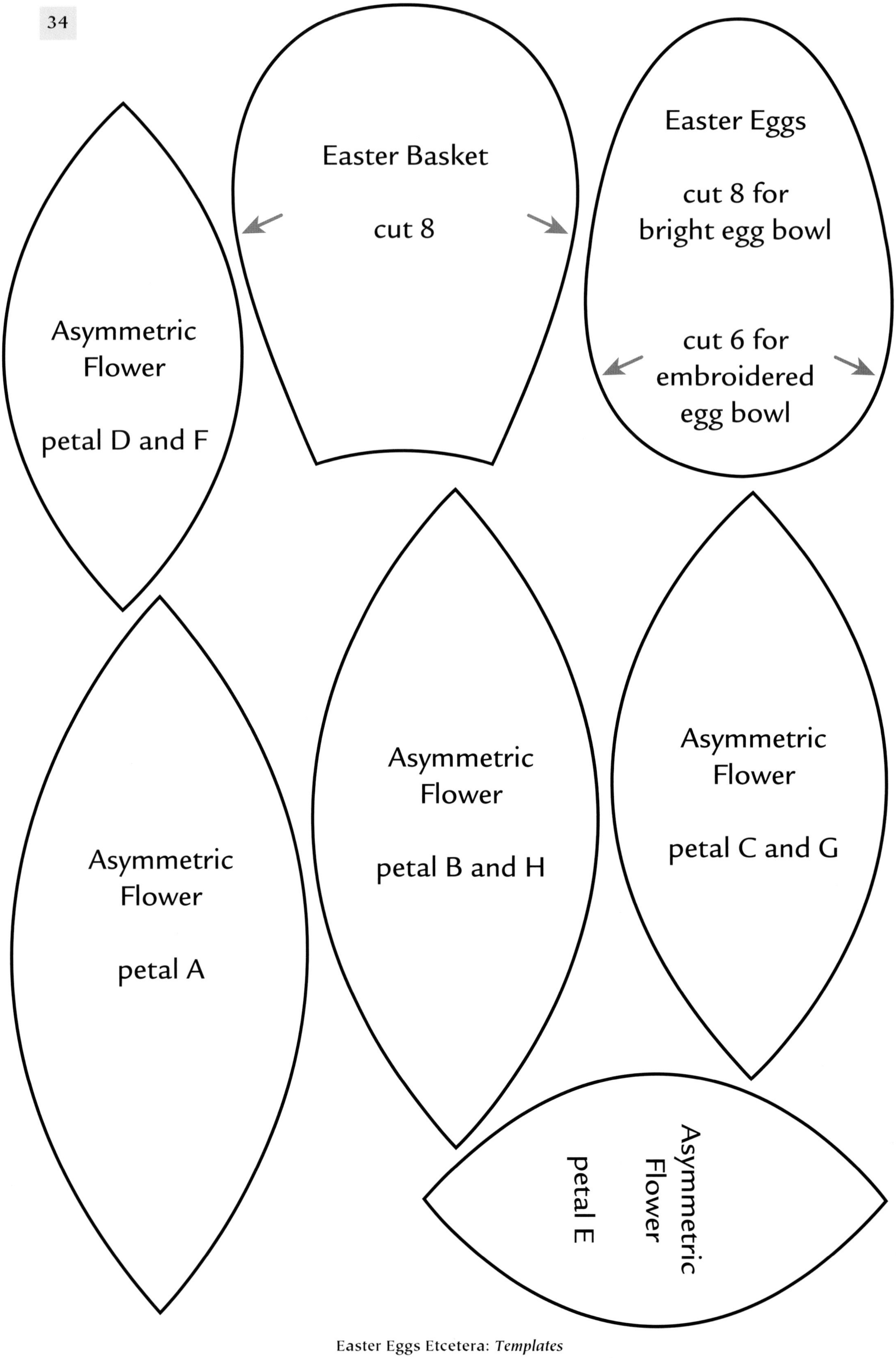

Asymmetric
Flower

petal D and F

Easter Basket

cut 8

Easter Eggs

cut 8 for
bright egg bowl

cut 6 for
embroidered
egg bowl

Asymmetric
Flower

petal A

Asymmetric
Flower

petal B and H

Asymmetric
Flower

petal C and G

Asymmetric
Flower

petal E

Easter Eggs Etcetera: *Templates*

The Seaside Collection

My husband Chris and I have a collection of shells we've picked up from beaches in different parts of the world – everything from a tiny butter-yellow shell from Tenby in Wales, to a green-lipped mussel shell from New Zealand! I'm lucky enough, too, to live quite near the seaside, and that's the inspiration for this collection of bowls.

Nautilus Shells

The gorgeous spirals of nautilus shells are very satisfying shapes, and I've used them to the full in the sides of this bowl. For the shells I used a batik printed with a tiny design of ferns; with the random colouring of the fabric background, it creates the impression of weathered shells covered with little strands of seaweed.

Difficulty rating ✪ ✪

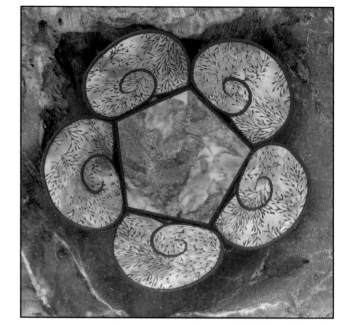

Materials

Option A, *if you're making all the shells from the same fabric, as I've done:*

- fusible interfacing:
  for the shells, one 24 x 5½in (61 x 14cm) strip
  for the base, one 7in (18cm) square

- fabrics:
  for the shells, two 24 x 5½in (61 x 14cm) strips
  for the centre, two 7in (18cm) squares

Option B, *if you're making each shell from a different fabric:*

- fusible interfacing:
  for the shells, five 5 x 5½in (13 x 14cm) patches
  for the base, one 7in (18cm) square

- fabrics:
  for the shells, ten 5 x 5½in (13 x 14cm) patches, two of each colour
  for the base, two 7in (18cm) squares

You will also need:

- Contrasting sewing thread
- Chalk marker

Instructions

1 **Option A** Prepare the strip of interfacing by fusing the strips of fabric onto it. Use the nautilus template on page 41 to mark five shell shapes, and cut them out in the usual way (**a**).

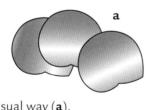

Option B Fuse the fabrics onto the individual patches of interfacing in matching pairs, then use the nautilus template on page 41 to mark one shell shape on each prepared patch. Cut out the shells.

2 Use the chalk marker to draw a spiral on each shell shape as shown on the template (**b**). Beginning at the point marked with a star on the template, work two layers

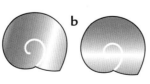

of satin stitch all around the edge of each patch and around the spiral (**c**), tapering the line towards the centre of the spiral.

3 Prepare the patch for the bowl base, then use pentagon template K on page 94 to mark the shape and cut it out (**d**). Work two layers of satin stitch around the central shape (**e**).

4 Lay the base on a flat surface and arrange the shells evenly around it (**f**); each shell will touch the base in two places. Pin firmly in position.

5 Join the bottom of each shell to the edge of the base with a few strong machine stitches; just stitch for about ⅓in (1cm) each time, otherwise the shell shapes will distort.

6 Pull the shell shapes up and join them where they touch, using the same technique.

TIP Try and keep the tapering spiral as smooth as possible as you stitch – try a couple of practice runs on some scrap fabric before you work on the shells themselves, so that you can get used to adjusting your machine's controls.

Starfish

A circle of starfish hold hands round this bowl; the template is cunningly designed so that as you join the arms of the starfish, the bowl shape is created. I used a single batik fabric in shades of blue, green and sand, which ensured that each starfish is unique while also creating a visual unity across the design.

Difficulty rating ✪ ✪ ✪

Materials

Option A, *if you're making all the starfish from the same fabric, as I've done:*

- fusible interfacing:
  for the starfish, one 26 x 6in (66 x 15cm) strip
  for the base, one 6in (15cm) square
- fabrics:
  for the starfish, two 26 x 6in (66 x 15cm) strips
  for the base, two 6in (15cm) squares of sandy fabric

Option B, *if you're making each starfish from a different fabric:*

- fusible interfacing:
  for the starfish, five 6in (15cm) square patches
  for the base, one 6in (15cm) square
- fabrics:
  for the starfish, ten 6in (15cm) square patches, two of each colour
  for the base, two 6in (15cm) squares of sandy fabric

You will also need:

- Contrasting sewing thread and sand-coloured thread
- Chalk marker

Instructions

1 **Option A** Prepare the strip of interfacing by fusing the strips of fabric onto it. Use the starfish template on page 42 to mark five shapes; use a dot or X of chalk to mark the top arm of each starfish, as shown on the template, then cut the shapes out in the usual way (**a**).

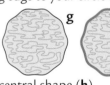

Option B Fuse the fabrics onto the individual patches of interfacing in matching pairs, then use the starfish template on page 42 to mark one shape on each prepared patch. Use a dot or X of chalk to mark the top arm of each starfish, as shown on the template, then cut the shapes out in the usual way.

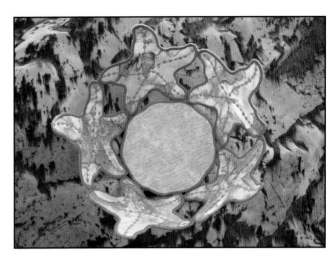

2 Use the chalk marker to draw central veins on each starfish shape

as shown on the template (**b**). Work lines of machine quilting or fancy embroidery stitches down each central vein (**c**). Beginning at the tip of a lower arm, work two layers of satin stitch all the way around each starfish shape (**d**).

3 Prepare the patch for the bowl base, then use centre template G on page 93 to mark the shape in chalk (**e**); cut it out, moving the scissors slightly inside and outside the marked line so that you end up with a gently waving edge to your circle (**f**).

4 Using a toning thread, free-machine quilt a wavy design across the base (**g**), then work two layers of satin stitch around the central shape (**h**).

5 Lay the base on a flat surface and arrange the starfish evenly around it (**i**); ensure that the top (marked) arm of each shape is furthest away from the base. Each starfish will touch the base in two places; pin firmly in position.

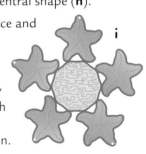

6 Join the the shapes to the base where the edges touch, using just a few strong machine stitches each time.

7 Pull the starfish shapes up into a bowl shape, and use the same technique to join the lower arms where they touch, just above the base. Once you've joined all the lower arms, join the upper arms in the same way.

TIP If you'd like a slightly simpler bowl, keep the base as a plain circle and omit its quilted decoration.

Scallops

Scallop shells have been used for centuries as decorative motifs; sometimes the shapes were stylised and carved into wood or plaster, and sometimes the shells themselves were used to decorate grottoes and summerhouses. For this bowl I've stitched a ring of scallop shells and overlapped them round a circular base.

Difficulty rating ✪ ✪ ✪

Materials

Option A, *if you're making all the shells from the same fabric, as I've done:*

- fusible interfacing:
  for the shells, one 16 x 11in (41 x 28cm) rectangle
  for the base, one 5½in (14cm) square

- fabrics:
  for the shells, two 16 x 11in (41 x 28cm) rectangles
  for the base, two 5½in (14cm) squares

Option B, *if you're making each shell from a different fabric:*

- fusible interfacing:
  for the shells, six 5½in (14cm) squares
  for the base, one 5½in (14cm) square

- fabrics:
  for the shells, twelve 5½in (14cm) squares, two of each colour
  for the base, two 5½in (14cm) squares

You will also need:

- Contrasting and toning sewing threads
- Chalk marker

Instructions

1 **Option A** Prepare the strip of interfacing by fusing the strips of fabric onto it. Use the scallop template on page 41 to mark six shell shapes, following the layout shown (**a**), then cut the shapes out in the usual way (**b**).

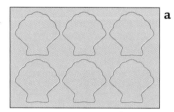

Option B Fuse the fabrics onto the individual patches of interfacing in matching pairs, then use the scallop template on page 41 to mark one shell shape on each prepared patch. Cut the shapes out in the usual way.

2 Use the chalk marker to draw the ridges and the central point on each scallop shape as shown on the template (**c**). Using toning thread, work lines of machine quilting down each ridge (**d**).

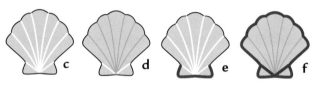

3 Work two layers of satin stitch round the bottom edge of each scallop shell (**e**). Then, beginning at the pointed tip of each shape, work two layers of satin stitch all the way around the remaining line (**f**).

4 Prepare the patch for the bowl base, then use centre template G on page 93 to mark the shape and cut it out (**g**). Work a double layer of satin stitch around the circle (**h**).

5 Lay the base on a flat surface and arrange the scallops evenly around it (**i**); pin firmly in position. Join the the shapes to the base where the edges touch, using hand or machine stitching.

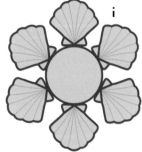

6 Pull the scallop shells up and overlap them so that they form a bowl shape; pin in place. On the outside of the bowl, slipstitch the shapes where they overlap.

TIP I used a mottled batik fabric for these shapes, which gave each shell its own character while keeping a sense of unity across the design.

Tropical Fish

Create your own school of dolphins, swimming in a circle round this bowl; the shapes are cut from a multicolored batik, which produces just the right exotic feel. Once the fish patches are joined to the base, you can pull them up and overlap them by different amounts depending on how deep you'd like the bowl to be.

Difficulty rating ✪ ✪

Materials

Option A, *if you're making all the fish from the same fabric, as I've done:*

- fusible interfacing:
  for the fish, one 17 x 6½in (43 x 16.5cm) strip
  for the base, one 5½in (14cm) square

- fabrics:
  for the fish, two 17 x 6½in (43 x 16.5cm) strips
  for the base, two 5½in (14cm) squares

Option B, *if you're making each fish from a different fabric:*

- fusible interfacing:
  for the fish, five 4 x 6½in (10 x 16.5cm) patches
  for the base, one 5½in (14cm) square

- fabrics:
  for the fish, ten 4 x 6½in (10 x 16.5cm) patches, two of each colour
  for the base, two 5½in (14cm) squares

You will also need:

- Contrasting sewing thread
- Ten small round beads for the eyes

Instructions

1 Option A
Prepare the strip of interfacing by fusing the strips of fabric onto it. Use the tropical

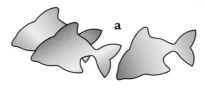

fish template on page 41 to mark five shapes, then cut the shapes out in the usual way (**a**).

Option B Fuse the fabrics onto the individual patches of interfacing in matching pairs, then use the tropical fish template on page 41 to mark one shape on each prepared patch. Cut the shapes out in the usual way.

2 Using a slightly narrower stitch than usual (as the patches are quite detailed), work two layers of satin stitch round all around the outside of each fish

shape (**b**). Begin and end the stitching line at the bottom tip of

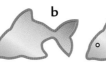

the tail. Add the beads for the eyes, stitching right through the patch each time (**c**).

3 Prepare the patch for the bowl base, then use centre template F on page 94 to mark

the shape and cut it out (**d**). Work two layers of satin stitch around the edge of the circle (**e**).

4 Lay the base on a flat surface and arrange the fish evenly around it (**f**); each fish will touch the base with its tail and its bottom fin. Pin firmly in position.

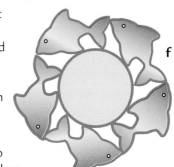

5 Join the the shapes to the base where the edges touch, using just a few strong stitches each time.

6 Pull the fish up and overlap them so that they form a bowl shape; pin in place. On the outside of the bowl, slipstitch the shapes where they overlap.

TIP Pick a thread colour that contrasts well with the colours in your fabric, so that the shapes remain distinct when they're overlapped.

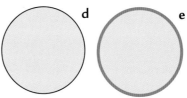

Under the Sea

I couldn't resist creating this fantasy bowl: brightly-coloured little fish swim in and out of a forest of seaweed strands. The seaweed shapes are fairly complex, and there are quite a few of them, which is what gives the bowl its five stars – if you decide to do this design it will take you a while, but the end result will be your own aquarium!

Difficulty rating ✪ ✪ ✪ ✪ ✪

Materials

- fusible interfacing:
  for the fish, one 15 x 4in (38 x 10cm) strip
  for the seaweed, one 25 x 5½in (64 x 14cm) strip
  for the base, one 4½in (11.5cm) square

- fabrics:
  for the fish, two 15 x 4in (38 x 10cm) strips
  for the seaweed, two 25 x 5½in (64 x 14cm) strips
  (or the equivalent in several different green fabrics)
  for the base, two 4½in (11.5cm) squares

You will also need:

- Black sewing thread
- Sixteen small round beads for the eyes

Instructions

1 Prepare the strip of interfacing for the fish by fusing on the appropriate strips of fabric. Use the small fish template on page 42 to mark eight shapes, then cut the shapes out in the usual way (**a**).

2 Prepare the strip for the strands of seaweed, then use the three seaweed templates on page 42 to mark ten shapes; to create plenty of variety, use the templates one way up for some of the strands and the other way up for others. Cut out the shapes (**b**).

3 Using a slightly narrower stitch than usual (as the patches are quite small and detailed), work two layers of satin stitch all around the outside of each fish shape (**c**) and each piece of weed (**d**).

4 Add the beads for the fishes' eyes, stitching right through the patch each time (**e**).

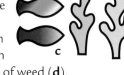

5 Prepare the patch for the bowl base, then use centre template D on page 92 to mark the shape and cut it out (**f**).

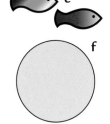

6 Lay the base on a flat surface and arrange the strands of seaweed around it (**g**); pin firmly in position. Work a double circuit of zigzag around the edge of the base, then trim the bottom of the seaweed shapes on the back of the work if necessary. Work a double layer of wider satin stitch all round the edge of the centre circle (**h**).

7 Pull the strands of seaweed up gently so that they form a bowl shape; you'll find that some of the strands will naturally butt up against each other. At these places, pin the strands together and then join them with a few strong machine stitches. (Don't worry if some of the strands don't naturally touch each other – don't force them. This is where the fish come into their own in the next step!)

8 Now arrange the fish so that they're swimming in and out of the strands of seaweed; use the fish to bridge any gaps between strands that you haven't been able to join. Slipstitch the shapes where they overlap.

TIP If you want to use a metallic fabric for the fish, as I've done, check whether you can iron directly onto it without it melting. If it tends to catch on the iron, use a non-stick pressing sheet between the iron and the fabric while you're fusing it in place.

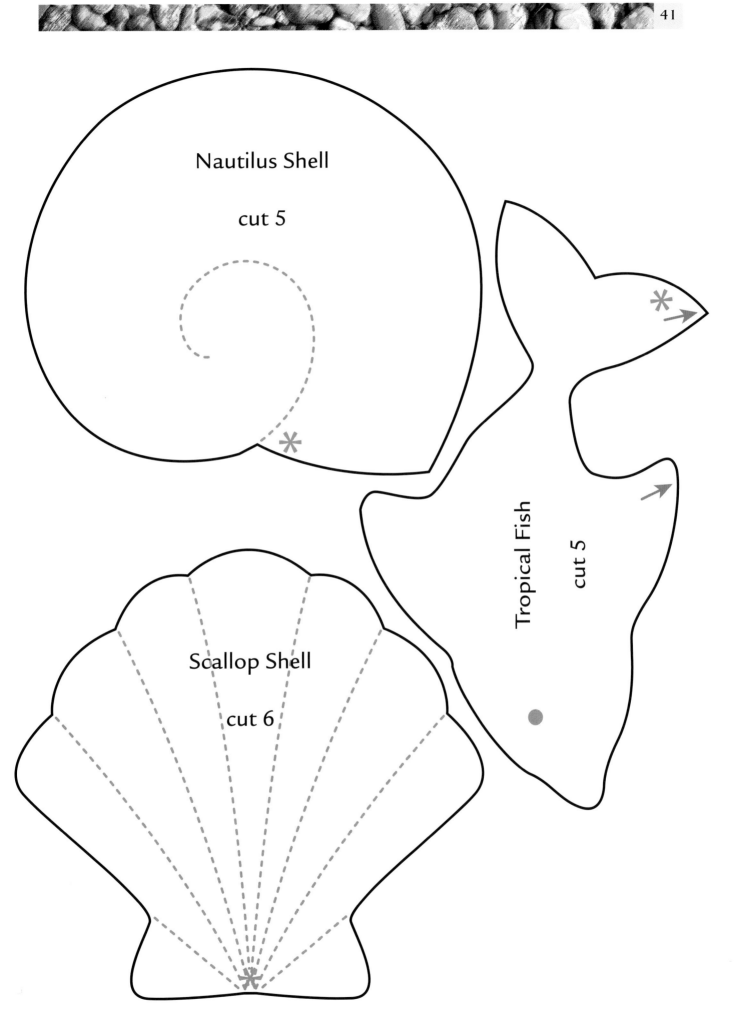

Nautilus Shell

cut 5

Tropical Fish

cut 5

Scallop Shell

cut 6

The Seaside Collection: *Templates*

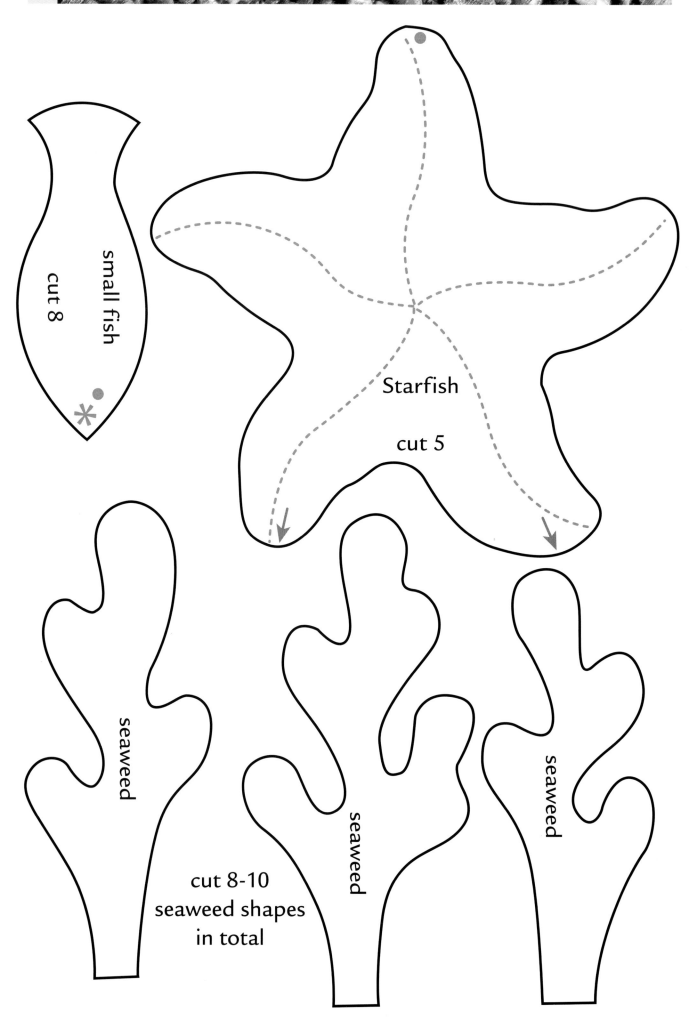

small fish

cut 8

Starfish

cut 5

seaweed

seaweed

seaweed

cut 8-10
seaweed shapes
in total

The Seaside Collection: *Templates*

The Great Outdoors

Leaves and flowers, fruit and fungi; the many faces of nature are featured in this collection of bowls. Pick soft woodland colours for subtle effects, or create a citrus fruit salad in bright batiks, and use the bowls to show off nature's bounty – seed-heads, acorns, dried flowers, pine-cones, pot pourri.

Green Leaves

Leaves come in all shapes and sizes, and if you like the idea of designing your own bowls, you'll discover lots of different ways in which you can combine their shapes! For this version, featuring gently pointed leaf shapes, I picked a different dusky green batik print for each patch to create the idea of a drift of leaves.

Difficulty rating ✪ ✪ ✪

Materials

***Option A**, if you're making all the leaves from the same fabric:*

- fusible interfacing:
  for the leaves, one 25 x 6in (64 x 15cm) strip
  for the base, one 5½in (14cm) square

- fabrics:
  for the leaves, two 25 x 6in (64 x 15cm) strips
  for the base, two 5½in (14cm) squares

***Option B**, if you're making each leaf in a different fabric, as I've done:*

- fusible interfacing:
  for the leaves, six 4½ x 6in (11.5 x 15cm) patches
  for the base, one 5½in (14cm) square

- fabrics:
  for the leaves, twelve 4½ x 6in (11.5 x 15cm) patches, two of each colour
  for the base, two 5½in (14cm) squares

You will also need:

- Contrasting sewing thread
- Chalk marker

Instructions

1 **Option A** Prepare the strip of interfacing by fusing one strip of fabric to each side. Use the leaf template on page 48 to mark six shapes, and cut them out in the usual way (**a**).

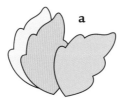

Option B Fuse the fabrics onto the individual patches of interfacing in matching pairs, then use the leaf template on page 48 to mark one shape on each prepared patch. Cut out the leaves.

2 Prepare the patch for the bowl base, then use centre template F on page 93 to mark the circle and cut it out (**b**).

3 Following the dotted line on the template, use chalk marker to draw in a vein line on each leaf shape (**c**). Work a line of satin stitch down this centre vein (**d**), tapering the line of stitching slightly towards the tip of each leaf; then, beginning at the base of each leaf, work two layers of satin stitch all around the edge of the leaf patches (**e**).

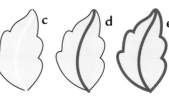

4 Work two layers of satin stitch all around the edge of the base circle (**f**). Lay the base on a flat surface and arrange the leaves evenly around it (**g**); the lower edge of each leaf will touch the base between the points marked by the green arrows on the template. Pin firmly in place.

5 Join the leaves to the edge of the base by hand or machine. Pull the leaf shapes up and pin them so that they touch at the points marked by the grey arrows on the template, then join the shapes with a few strong stitches by hand or machine.

TIP **Try fabrics in shades of gold and brown for an autumnal version of this bowl.**

Mushrooms

Stitch your own fairy ring of fungi, and maybe the little folk will come to visit ... A simple marbled fabric in a mushroomy colour is ideal for this bowl; the impression of a darker underside to the mushrooms is created with radiating lines of machine quilting. Small bug charms create the perfect finishing touch.

Difficulty rating ✪ ✪ ✪ ✪

Materials

- fusible interfacing:
  for the mushrooms, one 20 x 7in (51 x 18cm) strip
  for the base, one 5½in (14cm) square

- fabrics:
  for the mushrooms, two 20 x 7in (51 x 18cm) strips
  for the base, two 5½in (14cm) squares

You will also need:

- Dark brown sewing thread
- Chalk marker
- Two (or more) ladybird buttons, beads or charms

Instructions

1 Prepare the strip of interfacing by fusing one strip of fabric to each side. Use the two mushroom templates on page 49 to mark four large shapes and three small ones, and cut them out in the usual way. On

three of the large shapes and one of the small ones, use the chalk marker to draw in the top of the stalk and the underneath shape of the mushroom (**a**). On the remaining shapes, draw a line to join the edges of the mushroom cap as shown (**b**).

2 Working on the first set of shapes, stitch a radiating design of straight stitches on each mushroom to create gills (**c**). Now stitch a line of satin stitch around the outside of the gills, along the marked line (**d**). Stitch a double layer of satin stitch around the edge of the mushroom cap (**e**), then complete the shape by stitching around the edge of the stalk (**f**); don't stitch across the bottom of the stalk.

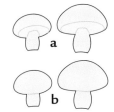

3 On the second set of shapes, stitch a double layer of satin stitch down each side of the stalk (**g**); don't

stitch across the bottom of the stalk. Now work a double layer of satin stitch all around the cap (**h**); if you begin at the top of one of your first lines of stitching, it will be easier to disguise the beginning and end of your stitching line.

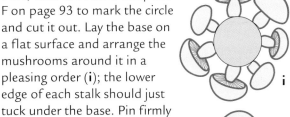

4 Prepare the patch for the bowl base, then use centre template F on page 93 to mark the circle and cut it out. Lay the base on a flat surface and arrange the mushrooms around it in a pleasing order (**i**); the lower edge of each stalk should just tuck under the base. Pin firmly in place.

5 Work two circuits of zigzag around the edge of the bowl base, then trim the ends of the stalks on the back of the work if necessary. Work a double layer of satin stitch all round the edge of the base circle (**j**). Pull the mushroom shapes up and pin them so that they overlap into a pleasing bowl shape, and pin firmly; slipstitch the overlaps on the outside of the bowl. Add a pair of ladybirds to one mushroom, stitching them right through the patch.

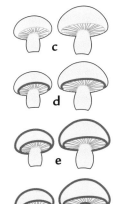

TIP If you want a circle of magic mushrooms (!) rather than realistic ones, cut them from bright, jazzy fabrics and prepare them all as described in step 3, to keep things simple.

St Clement's

'Oranges and lemons, say the bells of St Clement's'; so goes the old nursery rhyme, and for this design they're joined by bright green limes, too! I rather liked the play on words of making a 'fruit bowl' ... Batik fabrics in bright colours give the patches extra visual interest, and I found a batik for the base which picked up all the citrus colours.

Difficulty rating ✪ ✪ ✪

Materials

- fusible interfacing:

    for the oranges, one 13 x 4½in (33 x 11.5cm) strip

    for the lemons, one 10 x 5in (25 x 13cm) strip

    for the limes, one 7 x 3½in (18 x 9cm) strip

    for the base, one 5½in (14cm) square

- fabrics:

    for the oranges, two 13 x 4½in (33 x 11.5cm) strips of bright orange

    for the lemons, two 10 x 5in (25 x 13cm) strips of yellow

    for the limes, two 7 x 3½in (18 x 9cm) strips of lime green

    for the base, two 5½in (14cm) squares

You will also need:

- Brown sewing thread

Instructions

1 Prepare each strip of interfacing by fusing the strips of the appropriate fabric to each side. Use the lemon template on page 49 to mark and cut three shapes from the yellow strip (**a**). Use the lime template on page 49 to mark and cut three shapes from the green strip (**b**). Use the orange template on page 48 to mark and cut three shapes from the orange strip (**c**).

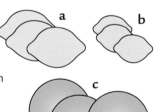

2 Prepare the patch for the bowl base, then use centre template F on page 93 to mark the circle and cut it out (**d**).

3 Work a double layer of satin stitch all around each fruit shape (**e**), and all around the edge of the base circle (**f**). Stitch a series of straight stitches in a star near the edge of each orange.

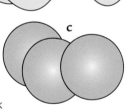

4 Lay the base on a flat surface and arrange the oranges at even intervals around it; pin firmly in place. In between each pair of oranges, arrange a lemon patch at a slight angle (**g**) and pin in place. Work a few strong machine stitches to join each shape to the base where the edges touch.

5 Pull the orange and lemon shapes up and overlap them to create a bowl shape; pin them firmly, then slipstitch the shapes on the back where they overlap. Now add the limes wherever they work well on your design, slipstitching them in place by hand.

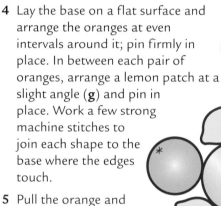

TIP Batiks and tiny prints work especially well for this bowl; they create a more natural look than solid fabrics or large prints.

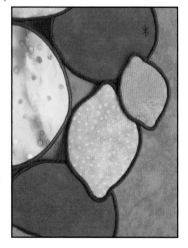

Flower Basket

This design creates the impression of a woven basket; the simple curved patches are overlapped around the centre of the bowl, then pulled up and slipstitched to form the basket shape. If you like, you could add a handle across the top as I've done for the Easter Basket (see page 32).

Difficulty rating ✪ ✪

Materials

- fusible interfacing:
  for the side pieces, one 21 x 8in (54 x 20cm) rectangle
  for the base, one 5½in (14cm) square

- fabrics:
  for the side pieces, two 21 x 8in (54 x 20cm) rectangles
  for the base, two 5½in (14cm) squares

You will also need:

- Contrasting sewing thread

Instructions

1 Prepare the strip of interfacing by fusing one strip of fabric to each side. Use the basket template on page 48 to mark nine horseshoe shapes, following the layout shown in the diagram (**a**), and cut them out in the usual way (**b**).

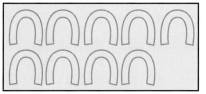

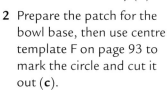

2 Prepare the patch for the bowl base, then use centre template F on page 93 to mark the circle and cut it out (**c**).

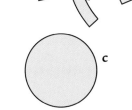

3 Work two layers of satin stitch round the inner and outer curves of the horseshoe-shaped patches (**d**); don't stitch across the short ends of the shapes.

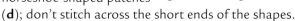

4 Lay the base on a flat surface and arrange the horseshoe shapes evenly around it; each shape should overlap the one next to it (**e**). Ease the ends of the shapes gently so that they fit the curve

of the base; this will make the shapes stand up slightly, and will create a good shape for the finished basket. Pin firmly in place, then stitch two circuits of zigzag around the edges of the centre circle. Trim the bottoms of the side shapes on the back of the work if necessary, then work two layers of satin stitch all around the edge of the base circle (**f**).

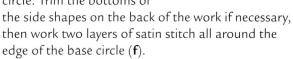

5 Pull up the side shapes so that they overlap and create an even bowl shape; pin them in place, then join the shapes by slipstitching the overlaps by hand on the outside of the bowl.

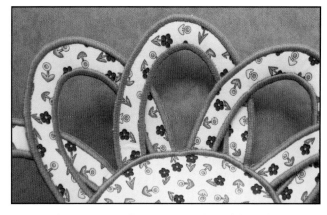

TIP Choose a small print or a plain fabric for this design; large prints will get lost on the narrow strips.

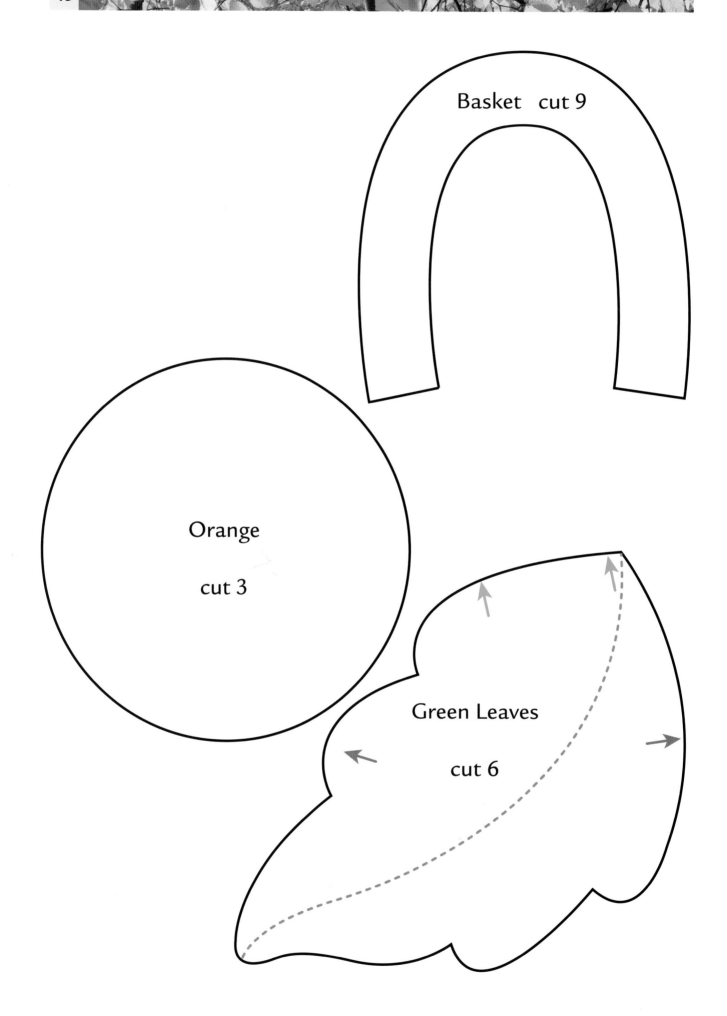

Basket   cut 9

Orange

cut 3

Green Leaves

cut 6

The Great Outdoors: *Templates*

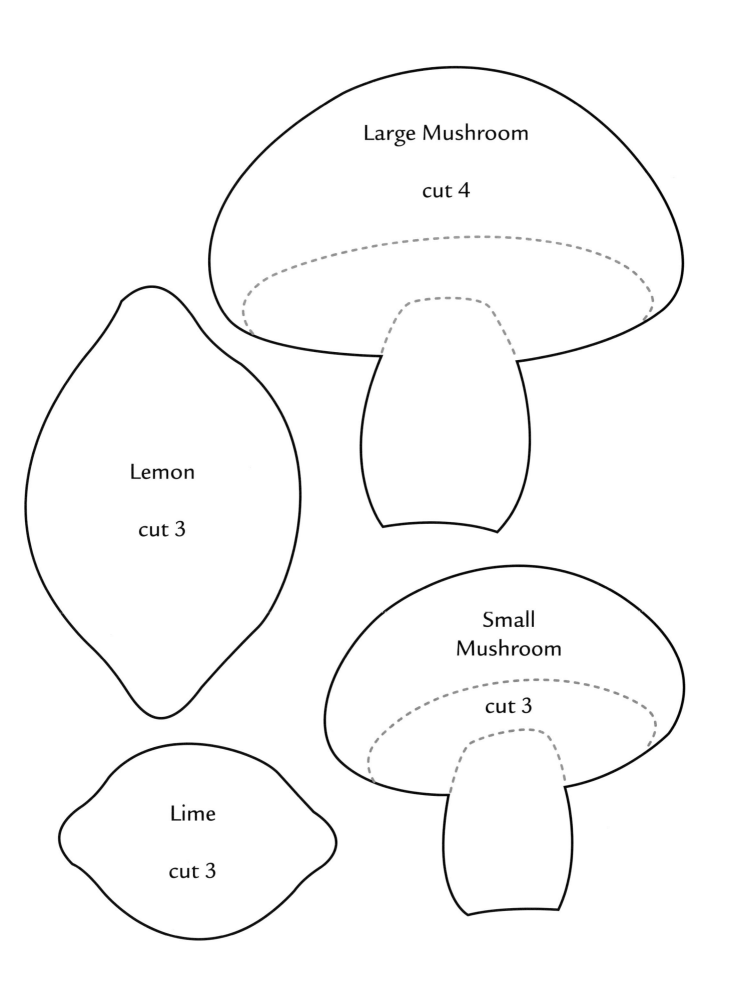

Large Mushroom

cut 4

Lemon

cut 3

Small
Mushroom

cut 3

Lime

cut 3

The Great Outdoors: *Templates*

The Chinese Collection

Oriental art has a wealth of beautiful, stylised motifs that lend themselves wonderfully to textile arts. In this collection I've taken a series of traditional Chinese motifs (fans, ginger jars, clouds, plum blossoms and butterflies) and designed a bowl to provide a fitting showcase for each shape.

Plum Blossom

The appearance of the plum blossom is a traditional sign of spring in the east, and streets lined with pale flowers draw as many crowds as the fall displays in Canada. Not surprisingly, the stylised plum blossom appears often in oriental art, and for this bowl I've echoed the very formal appearance of those graphic flower motifs.

Difficulty rating ✪ ✪

Materials

Option A, if you're making all the petals from the same fabric, as I've done:

- fusible interfacing:
  for the petals, one 22 x 4½in (56 x 11.5cm) strip
  for the base, one 4½in (11.5cm) square

- fabrics:
  for the petals, two 22 x 4½in (56 x 11.5cm) strips
  for the base, two 4½in (11.5cm) squares

Option B, if you're making each petal in a different fabric:

- fusible interfacing:
  for the petals, five 6 x 4½in (15 x 11.5cm) patches
  for the base, one 4½in (11.5cm) square

- fabrics:
  for the petals, ten 6 x 4½in (15 x 11.5cm) patches, two of each colour
  for the base, two 4½in (11.5cm) squares

You will also need:

- Contrasting sewing thread
- Five medium/large beads

Instructions

1 **Option A** Prepare the strip of interfacing by fusing one strip of fabric to each side. Use the petal template on page 56 to mark five petal shapes, and cut them out in the usual way (**a**).

Option B Fuse the fabrics onto the individual patches of interfacing in matching pairs, then use the petal template on page 56 to mark one shape on each prepared patch. Cut out the petals.

2 Prepare the patch for the bowl base, then use centre template D on page 92 to mark the circle and cut it out (**b**).

3 Work a few lines of straight machine stitching radiating out from the base of each petal (**c**).

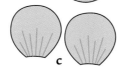

4 Work two layers of satin stitch round the curved edge of each petal (**d**); don't stitch across the bottom edges of the petals.

5 Lay the base circle on a flat surface and position the petals evenly around it (**e**) – don't panic: there are meant to be gaps between the bottoms of the petals! Pin firmly in place. Work two lines of zigzag all around the edge of the base circle.

6 Trim the bottoms of the petal shapes on the back of the work if necessary. Now work two layers of satin stitch all around the edges of the base circle (**f**).

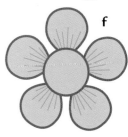

7 Pull up the petals to make a bowl shape, and join the petals by stitching a bead between each pair at the point indicated on the template.

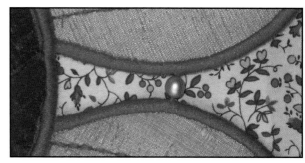

TIP If you prefer a slightly deeper bowl, pull the petals up so that they touch and join them with a few strong machine stitches instead of using beads.

Fans

The fan motif appears everywhere in oriental art; there's something very satisfying about its simple yet distinctive shape. For this design I've used a plain silk dupion decorated with patches of pink, but if you want to create a simpler bowl you can just cut the basic fan shapes from print fabrics and not bother adding the extra patches.

Difficulty rating ✪ ✪ ✪

Materials

- fusible interfacing:
  for the fans, one 22 x 5in (56 x 13cm) strip
  for the base, one 4½in (11.5cm) square

- fabrics:
  for the fans, two 22 x 5in (56 x 13cm) strips
  for the base, two 4½in (11.5cm) squares
  for the inside fan shapes, one 6 x 9in (15 x 23cm) rectangle

You will also need:

- Double-sided bonding web, one 6 x 9in (15 x 23cm) rectangle
- Contrasting sewing thread, plus toning thread for stitching the fan blades
- Five medium/large beads
- Chalk marker

Instructions

1 Prepare the strip of interfacing by fusing one strip of fabric to each side. Use the main fan template on page 57 to mark five large fan shapes, and cut them out in the usual way (**a**).

2 On the paper (smooth) side of the bonding web, trace the small inner fan template on page 57 ten times. Fuse the bonding web onto the back of the fabric you're using for the small fan shapes, then cut them out along the marked lines (**b**).

3 Peel the protective paper off the small fans and position them, web side down, on the large fan patches, matching the straight edges (**c**); fuse. Add a small fan to each side of every large fan shape.

4 On each fan, use the chalk marker to draw five straight lines as shown on the template. Work lines of straight stitch to produce the blades of the fans (**d**).

5 Work a line of satin stitch around the top curve of the inner fan shapes (**e**); as this is an internal line, you'll probably find that one line of stitching is enough.

6 Beginning at the points, work two layers of satin stitch all around each fan shape (**f**). Prepare the patch for the bowl base, then use centre template D on page 92 to mark the circle and cut it out. Work two layers of satin stitch all around the edge of the base (**g**).

7 Lay the base circle on a flat surface and position the fans evenly around it so that the tips just touch the edge of the circle (**h**). Pin firmly in place, then secure each fan tip to the edge of the centre with a few strong machine stitches.

8 Pull up the fans and overlap them to make a bowl shape; the more you overlap the fans, the steeper the bowl will be. Once you're happy with the shape, pin the fans together and join them by stitching a bead between the shapes where they overlap at the front.

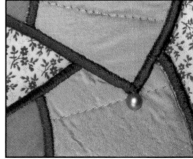

TIP I've just stitched my fans at one point where they overlap, using a bead to join the shapes; if you prefer a slightly firmer circle, you can slipstitch both points of each fan on the overlaps.

Oriental Clouds

Chinese and Japanese designers love incorporating stylised clouds in their work, and they produce unusual designs for stitchers to borrow! Here I've created a circle of clouds in white silk dupion, edged with royal blue to create a typical oriental colour-scheme; for the base I've used a pale blue silk as a contrast to the white.

Difficulty rating ✪ ✪ ✪ ✪

Materials

***Option A**, if you're making all the clouds from the same fabric, as I've done:*

* fusible interfacing:
  for the clouds, one 20 x 5½in (51 x 14cm) strip
  for the base, one 5½in (14cm) square
* fabrics:
  for the clouds, two 20 x 5½in (51 x 14cm) strips
  for the base, two 5½in (14cm) squares

***Option B**, if you're making each cloud in a different fabric:*

* fusible interfacing:
  for the clouds, five 4 x 5½in (10 x 14cm) patches
  for the base, one 5½in (14cm) square
* fabrics:
  for the clouds, ten 4 x 5½in (10 x 14cm) patches, two of each colour
  for the base, two 5½in (14cm) squares

You will also need:

* Contrasting sewing thread
* Chalk marker

Instructions

1 **Option A** Prepare the strip of interfacing by fusing one strip of fabric to each side. Use the cloud template on page 57 to mark five shapes, and cut them out in the usual way (**a**).

 Option B Fuse the fabrics onto the individual patches of interfacing in matching pairs, then use the cloud template on page 57 to mark one shape on each prepared patch. Cut out the clouds.

2 Prepare the patch for the bowl base, then use centre template F on page 93 to mark the circle and cut it out (**b**).

3 Following the dotted lines marked on the template, use chalk marker to draw in the spiral lines on each cloud shape (**c**).

4 Work two layers of satin stitch round the bottom curve of each cloud (**d**).  Then, beginning with a spiral, work two layers of satin stitch round the left-hand edge of each cloud shape (**e**). Finally, work a line of satin stitch around the remaining line on each cloud (**f**); begin and end with a spiral.

5 Work two layers of satin stitch all around the edge of the base circle (**g**). Lay the base on a flat surface and arrange the clouds evenly around it (**h**); the lower edges will touch the base at the points marked by the arrows on the template. Pin firmly in place.

6 Use a few strong machine stitches to secure these points to the edge of the base. Pull the cloud shapes up and pin them so that they overlap evenly; you can vary the depth of the bowl by altering the amount that you overlap the clouds. Once you're happy, slipstitch the shapes together on the outside of the bowl to secure them.

TIP **Practise the tapering satin stitch spirals on an offcut before you work on the final patches; that way, you get used to adjusting the control dials/buttons on your machine. If you find it too difficult to taper the spirals, just keep the width of the satin stitch the same throughout; your clouds will still look good!**

Butterflies

Delicate butterflies hover in a circle round this attractive bowl. I've made the butterflies from a single mottled blue fabric that also has a slight sparkle, and I've embellished each one with a different pattern of machine stitching; the base of the bowl is covered with a blue-and-white butterfly print to continue the theme.

Difficulty rating ✪ ✪ ✪ ✪

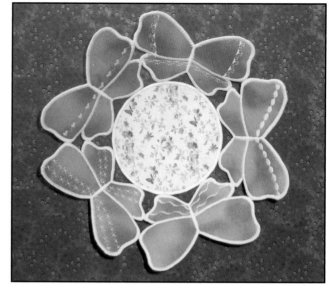

Materials

Option A, *if you're making all the butterflies from the same fabric, as I've done:*

* fusible interfacing:
  for the butterflies, one 23 x 5½in (59 x 14cm) strip
  for the base, one 5½in (14cm) square

* fabrics:
  for the butterflies, two 23 x 5½in (59 x 14cm) strips
  for the base, two 5½in (14cm) squares

Option B, *if you're making each butterfly in a different fabric:*

* fusible interfacing:
  for the butterflies, five 4½ x 5½in (11.5 x 14cm) patches
  for the base, one 5½in (14cm) square

* fabrics:
  for the butterflies, ten 4½ x 5½in (11.5 x 14cm) patches, two of each colour
  for the base, two 5½in (14cm) squares

You will also need:

* Contrasting sewing thread
* Chalk marker

Instructions

1 **Option A** Prepare the strip of interfacing by fusing one strip of fabric to each side. Use the butterfly template on page 56 to mark five shapes, and cut them out in the usual way (**a**).

   Option B Fuse the fabrics onto the individual patches of interfacing in matching pairs, then use the butterfly template on page 56 to mark one shape on each prepared patch. Cut out the butterflies.

2 Prepare the patch for the bowl base, then use centre template F on page 93 to mark the circle and cut it out (**b**).

3 Following the dotted lines marked on the template, use chalk marker to draw in the body and the wing line on each butterfly shape (**c**).

4 Use automatic machine stitches or free machining to embroider a design on each butterfly (**d**).

5 Work two layers of satin stitch round the edges of the bottom wings on each butterfly shape (**e**). Next, work two layers of satin stitch all round the upper wings (**f**); begin and end the line of stitching at the point marked by a star. Finally, work a line of satin stitch down the centre of each butterfly to create a body (**g**); taper the line a little at the top and bottom if you can, so that it looks more realistic.

6 Work two layers of satin stitch all around the edge of the base circle (**h**). Lay the base on a flat surface and arrange the butterflies evenly around it (**i**); the lower wings will touch the base at the points marked by the blue arrows on the template. Pin firmly in place.

7 Use a few strong machine stitches to secure these points to the edge of the base. Pull the butterfly shapes up and pin them so that the lower wings just touch at the points marked by the grey arrows on the template; join them with a few strong machine stitches. Finally, join the upper wings at the points marked by the pink arrows on the template.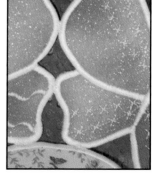

TIP For a simpler design, use a different bright print for each butterfly and omit the machine embroidery.

Ginger Jars

Ginger jars are very satisfying shapes: gently rounded and quite distinctive (rather like me, really ...) I've made each ginger jar from a different blue-and-white print, which looks very effective – although if you wanted to make them all from one fabric you could always decorate each jar with a different embroidered pattern or motif.

Difficulty rating ✪ ✪

Materials

Option A, if you're making all the jars from the same fabric:

- fusible interfacing:
  for the jars, one 21 x 4½in (53 x 11.5cm) strip
  for the base, one 4½in (11.5cm) square

- fabrics:
  for the jars, two 21 x 4½in (53 x 11.5cm) strips
  for the base, two 4½in (11.5cm) squares

Option B, if you're making each jar in a different fabric, as I've done:

- fusible interfacing:
  for the jars, six 3½ x 4½in (9 x 11.5cm) patches
  for the base, one 4½in (11.5cm) square

- fabrics:
  for the jars, twelve 3½ x 4½in (9 x 11.5cm) patches, two of each print
  for the base, two 4½in (11.5cm) squares

You will also need:

- Contrasting sewing thread
- Chalk marker

Instructions

1 **Option A** Prepare the strip of interfacing by fusing one strip of fabric to each side. Use the ginger jar template on page 56 to mark six shapes and cut them out in the usual way (**a**).

   Option B Fuse the fabrics onto the individual patches of interfacing in matching pairs, then use the ginger jar template on page 56 to mark one shape on each prepared patch. Cut out the jars.

2 Prepare the patch for the base, then use the centre template D on page 92 to mark the shape; cut it out (**b**).

3 Use the chalk marker to draw a line on the front of each jar shape (**c**); use the template as a guide for where the lines should go.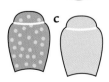

Stitch a line of satin stitch across this line on each shape (**d**) – one layer of stitching may well be enough, as it's an internal line.

4 Work two layers of satin stitch around the curved outside edges of the jars (**e**); don't stitch across the bottom edges of the shapes.

5 Lay the centre shape on a flat surface and arrange the jars evenly around it (**f**); the jar shapes should just touch each other, and will tuck slightly under the edges of the centre. Pin firmly in place.

6 Work two circuits of zigzag round the edge of the central shape to secure the jars, then trim the bottoms of the jar shapes on the back of the work if necessary. Work two circuits of satin stitch round the edges of the centre (**g**).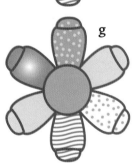

7 Pull the edges of the jars together and join them by machine to the point marked on the template.

TIP You don't have to use a blue-and-white colour-scheme for this design; ginger jars also come in green-and-white patterns – or you could use some of the opulent oriental prints on the market.

The Chinese Collection: *Ginger Jars*

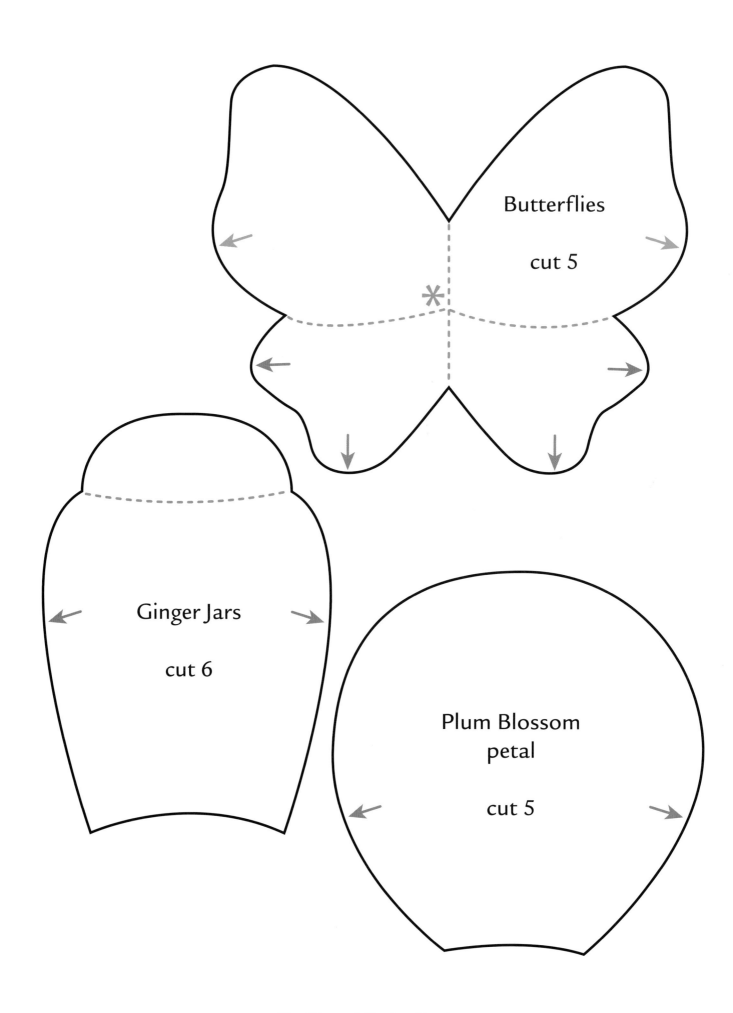

Butterflies

cut 5

Ginger Jars

cut 6

Plum Blossom
petal

cut 5

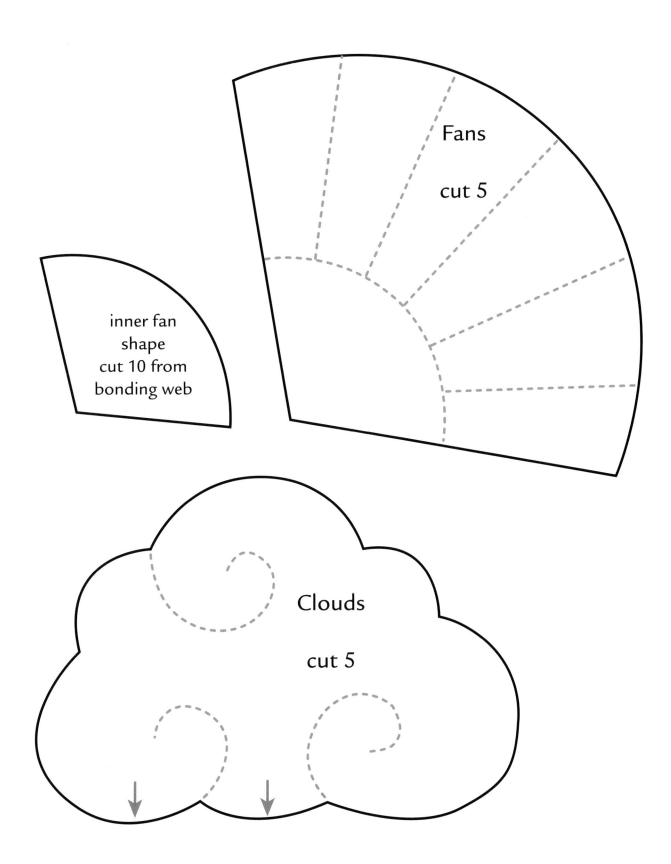

Fans

cut 5

inner fan
shape
cut 10 from
bonding web

Clouds

cut 5

The Chinese Collection: *Templates*

Jacobean Jewels

I've given these sumptuous bowls a Jacobean feel by making them in soft colours of silk and embroidering the patches with automatic machine stitching; the decorative black stitches produce an effect similar to blackwork embroidery. I first saw this idea on a quilt made by Stephanie Parker, so I'm indebted to her for the inspiration!

Embroidered Flower

To make the petals for this flower I used the technique described on pages 12-13 for decorating the covered strip of interfacing, but worked the lines of embroidery diagonally across the fabric. This way, each petal has a unique pattern of stitching across it, rather than all the petals being identical.

Difficulty rating ✪ ✪ ✪

Materials

- fusible interfacing:
  for the petals, one 24 x 6in (61 x 15cm) strip
  for the centre, one 3½in (9cm) square

- fabrics:
  for the petals, two 24 x 6in (61 x 15cm) strips
  for the centre, two 3½in (9cm) squares

You will also need:

- Black sewing thread
- Chalk marker and long quilt rule

Instructions

1 Prepare the strip of interfacing by fusing one strip of fabric to each side. Use the chalk marker and quilt rule to draw a line diagonally across the prepared strip. Draw other lines parallel to it at irregular intervals (**a**); the exact spacing of the lines doesn't matter. Work different automatic stitches across the design in black, following the marked lines and working between them if necessary; vary the stitches that you use, and the spaces between the lines (**b**).

Use the appropriate petal template on page 63 to mark six shapes, and cut them out in the usual way (**c**).

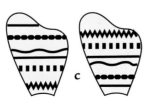

2 Work two layers of satin stitch around the curved edges of the petals (**d**); don't stitch across the bottom edges of the petal shapes.

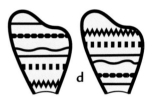

3 Prepare the patch for the flower centre, then use centre template B on page 92 to mark the shape; cut it out. Lay the centre shape on a flat surface and arrange the petals evenly around it (**e**); the petals should just touch each other, and will tuck slightly under the edges of the centre. Pin firmly in place.

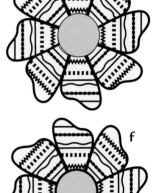

5 Work two circuits of zigzag round the edge of the central shape to secure the petals, then trim the bottoms of the petals on the back of the work if necessary. Work two circuits of satin stitch round the edges of the centre (**f**).

6 Pull the edges of the petals together and join them by machine to the point marked on the template.

TIP If you'd like all the petals of your flower to look the same, rather than featuring different patterns of stitching, work the lines of embroidery in straight lines down the prepared strip rather than diagonally across it.

Tulips

Tulips were favourite flowers in formal gardens during Jacobean and Elizabethan times, and – probably as a result – favourite decorative motifs inside the house too. Perhaps they liked the flowers' stately formality. In my version I've created a circle of formal embroidered tulip flowers, joined at the tips of the petals with beads.

Difficulty rating ✪ ✪ ✪ ✪

Materials

***Option A**, if you're making all the tulips from the same fabric, as I've done:*

- fusible interfacing:
  for the flowers, one 24 x 5in (61 x 13cm) strip
  for the base, one 4½in (11.5cm) square

- fabrics:
  for the flowers, two 24 x 5in (61 x 13cm) strips
  for the base, two 4½in (11.5cm) squares

***Option B**, if you're making each tulip in a different fabric:*

- fusible interfacing:
  for the flowers, six 4½ x 5in (11.5 x 13cm) patches
  for the base, one 4½in (11.5cm) square

- fabrics:
  for the flowers, twelve 4½ x 5in (11.5 x 13cm) patches, two of each colour
  for the base, two 4½in (11.5cm) squares

You will also need:

- Black sewing thread
- Chalk marker
- Six round beads and matching thread

Instructions

1 Option A Prepare the strip of interfacing by fusing one strip of fabric to each side. Use the tulip template on page 63 to mark six tulip shapes, and cut them out in the usual way (**a**).

Option B Fuse the fabrics onto the individual patches of interfacing in matching pairs, then use the tulip template on page 63 to mark one tulip shape on each prepared patch. Cut out the flowers.

2 Use the chalk marker to draw in the lines shown on the template (**b**). On each patch, using black thread, work a line of fancy machine stitching down the lines marked as pink on the template, and some free machining vermicelli/stipple quilting inside the top section (**c**).

3 Work two layers of satin stitch around the top curve of each tulip patch (**d**). Then, beginning at the position marked by the star on the template, stitch two layers of satin stitch all around the remaining marked lines and the outside of the tulip shape (**e**). Don't worry if the tips of your petals are a little bit untidy; they'll be neatened by the beads!

4 Prepare the patch for the bowl base, then use centre template D on page 92 to mark the circle and cut it out. Work two layers of satin stitch all around the edge of the base circle (**f**). If you like, decorate the centre with machine embroidery.

5 Lay the base on a flat surface and arrange the tulips evenly around it (**g**); the lower edge of each flower will just touch the edge of the base. Pin firmly in place, then join the edges with a few strong stitches by hand or machine.

6 Pull the tulip shapes up so that the curves of the outlines just touch, and join them with a few strong stitches. Finally, stitch a bead between each pair of tulips to join the petal tips.

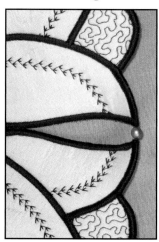

TIP If you prefer, join the tips of the tulip petals with a couple of firm hand stitches instead of using the beads.

Carnation

Carnations were popular Jacobean symbols too, and appear in many cross stitch samplers and fabric designs of the time. For this bowl I've taken a stylised carnation and embellished the petals with lines of embroidery to echo the pointed shapes. If you're lucky (!), the embroidery will create a star design within the flower.

Difficulty rating ✪ ✪ ✪

Materials

Option A, if you're making all the petals from the same fabric, as I've done:

- fusible interfacing:
  for the petals, one 24 x 6in (61 x 15cm) strip
  for the centre, one 3in (7.5cm) square

- fabrics:
  for the petals, two 24 x 6in (61 x 15cm) strips
  for the centre, two 3in (7.5cm) squares

Option B, if you're making each petal in a different fabric:

- fusible interfacing:
  for the petals, six 4½ x 6in (11.5 x 15cm) patches
  for the centre, one 3in (7.5cm) square

- fabrics:
  for the petals, twelve 4½ x 6in (11.5 x 15cm) patches, two of each colour
  for the centre, two 3in (7.5cm) squares

You will also need:

- Black sewing thread
- Chalk marker

Instructions

1 **Option A** Prepare the strip of interfacing by fusing one strip of fabric to each side. Use the carnation petal template on page 63 to mark six petal shapes and cut them out in the usual way (**a**).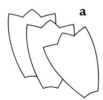

   Option B Fuse the fabrics onto the individual patches of interfacing in matching pairs, then use the carnation petal template on page 63 to mark one shape on each prepared patch. Cut out the petals.

2 On each petal shape, use the chalk marker to draw in the dotted lines shown on the template (**b**). Work a different fancy machine stitch along each line, then others between the lines if you wish (**c**).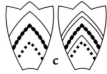

3 Work two layers of satin stitch around the main edges of the petals (**d**); don't stitch across the bottom edges of the petal shapes.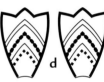

4 Prepare the patch for the flower centre, then use centre template A on page 92 to mark the shape; cut it out. I embellished the centre with some simple vermicelli/stipple quilting as a contrast to the more formal stitches (**e**).

5 Lay the centre shape on a flat surface and arrange the petals evenly around it (**f**); the petals should just touch each other, and will tuck slightly under the edges of the centre. Pin firmly in place.

6 Work two circuits of zigzag round the edge of the central shape to secure the petals, then trim the bottoms of the petals on the back of the work if necessary. Work two circuits of satin stitch round the edges of the centre (**g**).

7 Pull the edges of the petals together and join them by machine to the point marked on the template.

TIP This design would work well in pink, pale blue or mauve, too.

Pomegranates

*Pomegranates are often seen as symbols of fertility –
something to do with all those seeds spilling out of the split
fruit, perhaps. They also often feature in Jacobean crewel
work and other embroidery techniques, so it seemed just
right for this section to design a bowl featuring a ring
of decorative pomegranate fruits.*

Difficulty rating ✪ ✪ ✪ ✪

Materials

Option A, *if you're making all the pomegranates from the
same fabric, as I've done:*

- fusible interfacing:
  for the fruit, one 23 x 5in (59 x 13cm) strip
  for the base, one 5½in (14cm) square

- fabrics:
  for the fruit, two 23 x 5in (59 x 13cm) strips
  for the base, two 5½in (14cm) squares

Option B, *if you're making each pomegranate in a different
fabric:*

- fusible interfacing:
  for the fruit, six 4 x 5in (10 x 13cm) patches
  for the base, one 5½in (14cm) square

- fabrics:
  for the fruit, twelve 4 x 5in (10 x 13cm) patches,
  two of each colour
  for the base, two 5½in (14cm) squares

You will also need:

- Black sewing thread
- Chalk marker and ruler

Instructions

1 **Option A** Prepare the strip of interfacing by
fusing one strip of fabric to each side. Use the
pomegranate template on page 63 to mark six
shapes, and cut them out in the usual way (**a**).

   Option B Fuse the fabrics onto the individual
patches of interfacing in matching pairs, then use
the pomegranate template on page 63 to mark one
pomegranate shape on each prepared patch. Cut
out the fruit.

2 Use the chalk marker to draw in
the lines shown on the template
(**b**). On each patch, using black
thread, work a line of fancy
machine stitching down the lines marked as green
on the template, and lines of straight stitch across
the lattice design in the centre (**c**).

3 Work a line of satin stitch down the
inside curves of each pomegranate
patch (**d**). Then, beginning at the
base, work a double layer of satin
stitch all around the outside of each fruit shape (**e**).

4 Prepare the patch for
the bowl base, then use
hexagon template H on
page 93 to mark the
shape and cut it out (**f**).
Use the chalk marker to draw in a
lattice design across the base as shown
(**g**) – create this by joining opposite
corners first, then drawing in parallel
lines each side of each long line. Work
lines of straight stitch along all the marked lines (**h**).

5 Trim the corners of the hexagon
slightly to round them, then work two
layers of satin stitch all around the
edge of the base shape (**i**).

6 Lay the base on a flat
surface and arrange the
pomegranates evenly
around it (**j**); the lower edge
of each fruit will just touch
the edge of the base. Pin
firmly in place, then join the
edges with a few strong
stitches by hand or machine.

7 Pull the fruit shapes up so that the curves of the outlines
just touch, and join them with a few strong stitches.

TIP If you like, add a round black bead to the top of
each pomegranate shape for extra embellishment.

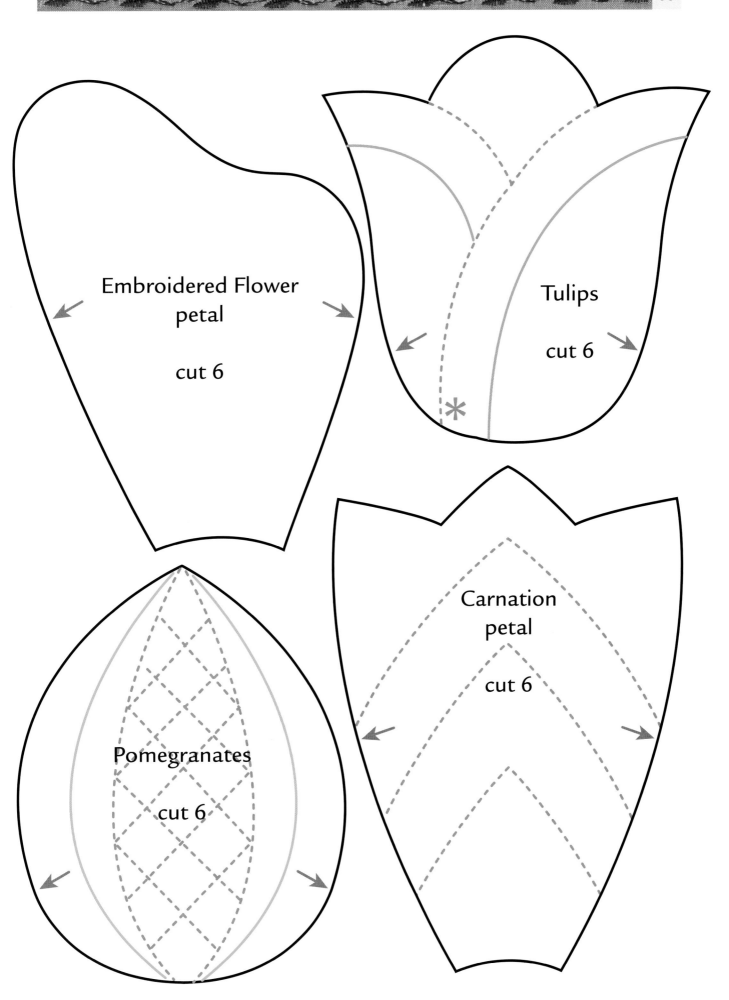

Embroidered Flower
petal

cut 6

Tulips

cut 6

Pomegranates

cut 6

Carnation
petal

cut 6

Jacobean Jewels: *Templates*

Fields and Hedgerows

Pretty in pinks, reds and yellows; these delicate flower bowls conjure up the hedgerows and verges in spring and summer. Two of the flowers are created in the traditional way, with separate petals joined where they touch, but for the poppy and briar rose I've overlapped the petals to give them a more realistic appearance.

Primrose

*Clumps of primroses are the first real herald of spring:
capture the moment with this delicate design. For this bowl
I thought I'd try a slightly unusual centre shape, which
echoes the pale green star shape you can see at the centre
of real primroses. The petals fit snugly round it, then are
pulled up and joined in the usual way.*

Difficulty rating ✿

Materials

*Option A, if you're making all the petals from the same
fabric, as I've done:*

- fusible interfacing:

  for the petals, one 16 x 4½in (41 x 11.5cm) strip

  for the centre, one 3in (7.5cm) square

- fabrics:

  for the petals, two 16 x 4½in (41 x 11.5cm) strips of
  pale yellow

  for the centre, two 3in (7.5cm) squares of pale green

Option B, if you're making each petal in a different fabric:

- fusible interfacing:

  for the petals, five 3½ x 4½in (9 x 11.5cm) patches

  for the centre, one 3in (7.5cm) square

- fabrics:

  for the petals, ten 3½ x 4½in (9 x 11.5cm) patches,
  two of each fabric

  for the centre, two 3in (7.5cm) squares of pale green

You will also need:

- Bright yellow sewing thread

Instructions

1 **Option A** Prepare the
strip of interfacing by
fusing one strip of yellow
fabric to each side. Use
the appropriate template
on page 69 to mark five
petal shapes and cut them
out in the usual way (**a**).

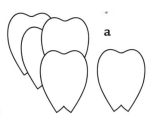

  Option B Fuse the fabrics onto the individual patches
of interfacing in matching pairs, then use the
appropriate template on page 69 to mark one petal
shape on each prepared patch. Cut out the petals.

2 Prepare the patch for the flower centre,
then use the centre template on page 69
to mark the shape; cut it out (**b**).

3 Work two layers of satin stitch
around the curved edges of
the petals (**c**); don't stitch
across the bottom edges of
the petal shapes.

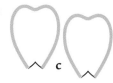

4 Lay the centre shape on a flat surface and arrange
the petals evenly around it (**d**); the petals should just
touch each other, and will tuck slightly under the
edges of the centre. Pin firmly in place.

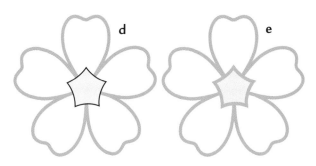

5 Work two circuits of zigzag round the edge of the
central shape to secure the petals, then trim the
bottoms of the petals on the back of the work if
necessary. Work two circuits of satin stitch round
the edges of the centre (**e**).

6 Pull the edges of the petals together and join them
by machine to the point marked on the template.

TIP If you prefer a slightly flatter bowl you could
make the lines of stitching a bit shorter, but don't
join the edges further up than the marked point,
otherwise the petals will start to pull out of shape.

Campion

Pink and white campions dot the hedgerows from spring till summer; when I was looking at photographs before I designed this bowl, I discovered that they come in far more shapes and sizes than I'd realised. I based my design on one of the flowers with long petals, because it was an unusual shape, but you could make your petals shorter if you prefer.

Difficulty rating ✪ ✪

Materials

Option A, *if you're making all the petals from the same fabric, as I've done:*

- fusible interfacing:
  for the petals, one 21 x 6in (54 x 15cm) strip
  for the centre, one 3in (7.5cm) square

- fabrics:
  for the petals, two 21 x 6in (54 x 15cm) strips of pale pink
  for the centre, two 3in (7.5cm) squares of pale green or yellow

Option B, *if you're making each petal in a different fabric:*

- fusible interfacing:
  for the petals, five 5 x 6in (13 x 15cm) patches
  for the centre, one 3in (7.5cm) square

- fabrics:
  for the petals, ten 5 x 6in (13 x 15cm) patches, two of each fabric
  for the centre, two 3in (7.5cm) squares of pale green or yellow

You will also need:

- Dark pink sewing thread

Instructions

1 **Option A** Prepare the strip of interfacing by fusing one strip of pink fabric to each side. Use the appropriate template on page 69 to mark five petal shapes and cut them out in the usual way (**a**).

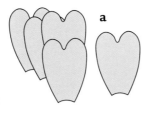

Option B Fuse the fabrics onto the individual patches of interfacing in matching pairs, then use the appropriate template on page 69 to mark one petal shape on each prepared patch. Cut out the petals.

2 Use the pink thread to work random lines of straight stitch across the petals from bottom to top (**b**).

3 Prepare the patch for the flower centre, then use the centre template B on page 92 to mark the central circle; cut it out.

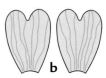

4 Work two layers of satin stitch around the curved edges of the petals (**c**); don't stitch across the bottom edges of the petal shapes.

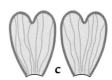

5 Lay the centre circle on a flat surface and arrange the petals evenly around it (**d**); the petals should just touch each other, and will tuck slightly under the edges of the centre. Pin firmly in place.

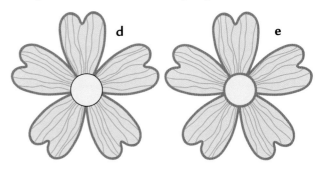

6 Work two circuits of zigzag round the edge of the central shape to secure the petals, then trim the bottoms of the petals on the back of the work if necessary. Work two circuits of satin stitch round the edges of the centre (**e**).

7 Pull the edges of the petals together and join them by machine to the point marked on the template; don't join the edges much further up than the marked point, otherwise the petals will start to pull out of shape.

TIP If you'd like to make a campion flower with shorter petals, cut the template down as shown.

Briar Rose

The thin, papery petals of these wild roses vary in colour from mid pink through to almost white, contrasting with the rich yellow stamens in the flower centres. To make the flower shape look realistic on this bowl I've stitched some extra details on the petals, then overlapped them round an oval base.

Difficulty rating ✿ ✿ ✿

Materials

- fusible interfacing:
  for the petals, one 19 x 4½in (48 x 11.5cm) strip
  for the centre, one 2½ x 3in (6.5 x 7.5cm) patch

- fabrics:
  for the petals, two 19 x 4½in (48 x 11.5cm) strips of white or very pale pink
  for the centre, two 2½ x 3in (6.5 x 7.5cm) patches of pale yellow

You will also need:

- Pale pink and bright yellow sewing threads
- Fabric crayons in pale pink and yellow
- Pink pencil crayon

Instructions

1 Prepare the strip of interfacing by fusing one strip of fabric to each side. Use the appropriate template on page 69 to mark five petal shapes and cut them out in the usual way (**a**).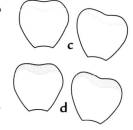

2 Now trim each petal shape slightly unevenly, so that all the petals end up slightly different (**b**).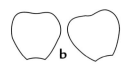

3 Use the pink pencil crayon to draw in a curved line at the top of each petal as shown (**c**); once again, make the shape on each petal slightly different. Use the pale pink fabric crayon to shade gently inside each shape (**d**).

4 Using the pale yellow fabric crayon, shade the bottom of each petal gently (**e**). Work some lines of yellow straight stitch across the bottom edge of each petal; make the lines random heights, radiating outwards slightly across the shape (**f**).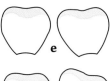

5 Work satin stitch round each of your drawn curves at the tops of the petals (**g**); you may well find that you only need one layer of satin stitch for these lines. Next, work two layers of satin stitch round the shaped outsides of the petals (**h**); don't stitch across the bottoms of the petals.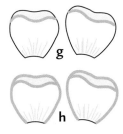

6 Prepare the patch for the flower centre, then use the oval centre template on page 69 to mark the shape; cut it out (**i**).

7 Lay the centre shape on a flat surface and arrange the petals around it (**j**); the petals should overlap each other randomly, and tuck slightly under the edges of the central oval. Pin firmly in place.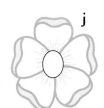

8 Work two circuits of zigzag round the edge of the central shape to secure the petals, then trim the bottoms of the petals on the back of the work if necessary. Work two circuits of satin stitch round the edges of the centre (**k**).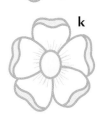

9 Pull the edges of the petals up gently to make a shallow bowl shape and pin them in place. Stitch the overlaps invisibly by hand on the outside of the bowl.

TIP Use fabric crayons in subtle colours to create the shaded areas; if your fabric crayons are all bright, try a dilute wash of fabric paint instead.

Poppy

From Monet onwards, poppies seem to have captured the romantic imagination, immortalised in numerous paintings and photographs; perhaps it's the blazing scarlet colour that makes our hearts beat that little bit faster. Now you can make your own poppy – a bright patch of colour that will brighten up even the dullest day

Difficulty rating ✪ ✪

Materials

Option A, *if you're making all the petals from the same fabric, as I've done:*

- fusible interfacing:
  for the petals, one 19 x 4in (48 x 10cm) strip
  for the centre, one 3in (7.5cm) square

- fabrics:
  for the petals, two 19 x 4in (48 x 10cm) strips of mottled red
  for the centre, two 3in (7.5cm) squares of mottled black

Option B, *if you're making each petal in a different fabric:*

- fusible interfacing:
  for the petals, five 4in (10cm) squares
  for the centre, one 3in (7.5cm) square

- fabrics:
  for the petals, ten 4in (10cm) squares, two of each fabric
  for the centre, two 3in (7.5cm) squares of mottled black

You will also need:

- Black sewing thread

Instructions

1 **Option A** Prepare the strip of interfacing by fusing one strip of red fabric to each side. Use the appropriate template on page 69 to mark five petal shapes and cut them out in the usual way (**a**).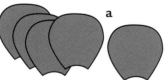

   Option B Fuse the fabrics onto the individual patches of interfacing in matching pairs, then use the appropriate template on page 69 to mark one petal shape on each prepared patch. Cut out the petals.

2 Now trim each petal shape slightly unevenly, so that all the petals end up slightly different (**b**).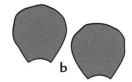

3 Prepare the patch for the flower centre, then use the centre template A on page 92 to mark the shape; cut it out (**c**).

4 Use a suitable automatic stitch or straight stitch to work black stamens radiating out from the bottom of each petal. Make the stamens different lengths for visual interest (**d**).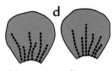

5 Work two layers of satin stitch around the curved edges of the petals (**e**); don't stitch across the bottom edges of the petal shapes.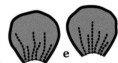

6 Lay the centre circle on a flat surface and arrange the petals around it (**f**); the petals should overlap each other randomly, and tuck slightly under the edges of the central shape. Pin firmly in place.

7 Work two circuits of zigzag round the edge of the central circle to secure the petals, then trim the bottoms of the petals on the back of the work if necessary. Work two circuits of satin stitch round the edges of the centre (**g**).

8 Pull the edges of the petals up gently to make a shallow bowl shape and pin them in place. Stitch the overlaps invisibly by hand on the outside of the bowl.

TIP I used an automatic stitch on my machine to create the black stamens, but you could use lines of straight machine stitching instead.

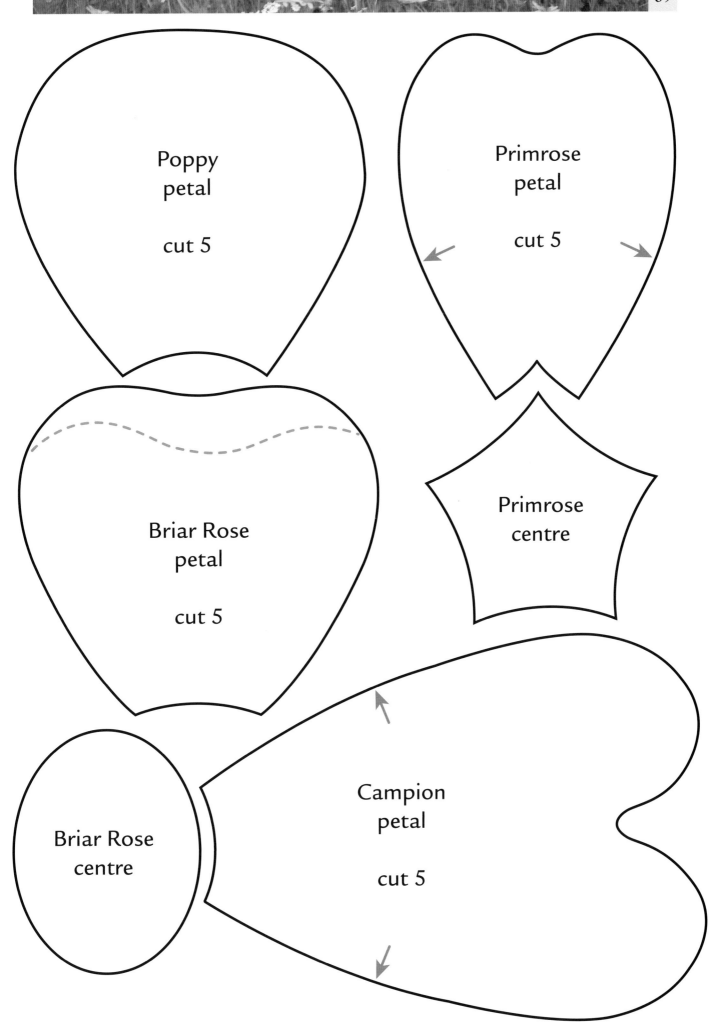

Poppy
petal

cut 5

Primrose
petal

cut 5

Briar Rose
petal

cut 5

Primrose
centre

Briar Rose
centre

Campion
petal

cut 5

Fields and Hedgerows: *Templates*

Art Deco Delights

The sculpted forms of the Art Deco movement provided the inspiration for this collection.
The strong geometric shapes used by the designers of the 1920s and 30s lend themselves perfectly
to constructing bowls, where the different planes have to fit together to create 3D shapes,
and I've added machine embroidery to a couple of the designs to emphasise the lines.

Embroidered Triangle

This small bowl is constructed from just three sides, stitched round a triangular base. I've echoed the curved edges of the side pieces with lines of machine embroidery; if you'd like to do the same, cut out the side pieces first, as it's easier to keep the curves smooth on a small piece of work.

Difficulty rating ✪ ✪

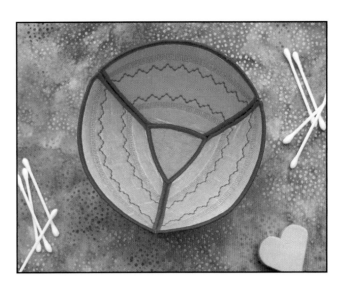

Materials

***Option A**, if you're making all the sides from the same fabric, as I've done:*

- fusible interfacing:
  for the sides, one 12 x 6½in (30 x 16.5cm) strip
  for the base, one 2½in (6.5cm) square

- fabrics:
  for the sides, two 12 x 6½in (30 x 16.5cm) strips
  for the base, two 2½in (6.5cm) squares

***Option B**, if you're making each side in a different fabric:*

- fusible interfacing:
  for the sides, three 4 x 6½in (10 x 16.5cm) patches
  for the base, one 2½in (6.5cm) square

- fabrics:
  for the sides, six 4 x 6½in (10 x 16.5cm) patches, two of each colour
  for the base, two 2½in (6.5cm) squares

You will also need:

- Contrasting sewing threads
- Chalk marker

Instructions

1 **Option A** Prepare the strip of interfacing by fusing one strip of fabric to each side. Use the relevant template on page 76 to mark three side shapes and cut them out in the usual way (**a**).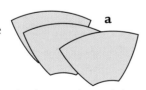

Option B Fuse the fabrics onto the individual patches of interfacing in matching pairs, then use the relevant template on page 76 to mark one side shape on each prepared patch. Cut out the shapes.

2 If you'd like to embroider the side pieces, work a few lines of embroidery across each patch, echoing the curves of the top and bottom (**b**).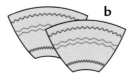

To help you keep the curves smooth, draw the lines in with chalk marker first; you can then use the lines as stitching guides.

3 Prepare the patch for the bowl base, then use the triangular centre template on page 76 to mark the shape; cut it out (**c**).

4 Work two layers of satin stitch over the short edges of the side patches (**d**); for this design, don't stitch across the long curve at the top of each patch, or across the bottom edge.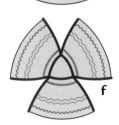

5 Lay the centre shape on a flat surface and arrange the sides evenly around it (**e**); the sides should just touch each other, and will tuck slightly under the edges of the centre. Pin firmly in place.

6 Work two circuits of zigzag round the edge of the central shape to secure the side pieces, then trim the bottoms of the side pieces on the back of the work if necessary. Work two circuits of satin stitch round the edges of the centre (**f**).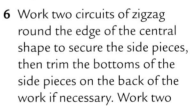

7 Pull the edges of the bowl sides together and join them by hand; this bowl is too steep to join the edges by machine. Once the sides are joined, trim the tops of the joins level if necessary, then work two circuits of satin stitch all the way around the top of the bowl. This produces a neater top than doing the long edges before you join the bowl.

TIP For a shallower bowl, extend the sides of the template a little so that the edges won't be so steep when you join them.

Curved Square

One of the simplest designs in the book – but no less effective for that! The sides of this bowl are made from the same template as the Embroidered Triangle design on page 71, but by using four side pieces round a square base you can produce a finished bowl that looks quite different.

Difficulty rating ✪

Materials

Option A, *if you're making all the sides from the same fabric, as I've done:*

- fusible interfacing:
  for the sides, one 17 x 6½in (43 x 16.5cm) strip
  for the base, one 3½in (9cm) square

- fabrics:
  for the sides, two 17 x 6½in (43 x 16.5cm) strips
  for the base, two 3½in (9cm) squares

Option B, *if you're making each side in a different fabric:*

- fusible interfacing:
  for the sides, four 4½ x 6½in (11.5 x 16.5cm) patches
  for the base, one 3½in (9cm) square

- fabrics:
  for the sides, eight 4½ x 6½in (11.5 x 16.5cm) patches, two of each colour
  for the base, two 3½in (9cm) squares

You will also need:

- Contrasting sewing thread

Instructions

1 **Option A** Prepare the strip of interfacing by fusing one strip of fabric to each side. Use the relevant template on page 76 to mark four side shapes and cut them out in the usual way (**a**).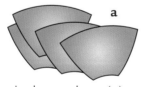

   Option B Fuse the fabrics onto the individual patches of interfacing in matching pairs, then use the relevant template on page 76 to mark one side shape on each prepared patch. Cut out the shapes.

2 Prepare the patch for the bowl base, then use the square centre template on page 76 to mark the shape; cut it out (**b**).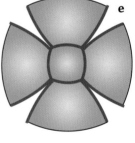

3 Work two layers of satin stitch over the short edges of each side patch (**c**); for this design, don't stitch across the long curve at the top of each patch, or across the bottom edge.

4 Lay the centre shape on a flat surface and arrange the sides evenly around it (**d**); the sides should just touch each other, and will tuck slightly under the edges of the centre. Pin firmly in place.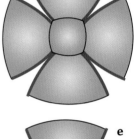

5 Work two circuits of zigzag round the edge of the central shape to secure the side pieces, then trim the bottoms of the side pieces on the back of the work if necessary. Work two circuits of satin stitch round the edges of the centre square (**e**).

6 Pull the edges of the bowl sides together and join them by hand or machine. Once the sides are joined, trim the tops of the joins level if necessary, then work two circuits of satin stitch all the way around the top of the bowl. Leaving the top edge till last creates a smoother finish to the bowl.

TIP The sides of this bowl are large enough to show off quite an ornate print; I picked quite a complex print fabric, then chose a single motif from it as a focus for the base of the bowl.

Art Deco Delights: *Curved Square*

Wavy Square

For this design I've adapted the Curved Square bowl opposite, using the same shape for the base of the bowl but altering the side shapes so that they're wavy at the top. I've then echoed the wavy silhouette with a line of machine embroidery, which creates a simple but attractive border.

Difficulty rating ✪ ✪

Materials

Option A, *if you're making all the sides from the same fabric, as I've done:*

- fusible interfacing:
  for the sides, one 17 x 6½in (43 x 16.5cm) strip
  for the base, one 3½in (9cm) square

- fabrics:
  for the sides, two 17 x 6½in (43 x 16.5cm) strips
  for the base, two 3½in (9cm) squares

Option B, *if you're making each side in a different fabric:*

- fusible interfacing:
  for the sides, four 4½ x 6½in (11.5 x 16.5cm) patches
  for the base, one 3½in (9cm) square

- fabrics:
  for the sides, eight 4½ x 6½in (11.5 x 16.5cm) patches, two of each colour
  for the base, two 3½in (9cm) squares

You will also need:

- Contrasting sewing thread
- Chalk marker

Instructions

1 **Option A** Prepare the strip of interfacing by fusing one strip of fabric to each side. Use the relevant template on page 76 to mark four side shapes and cut them out in the usual way (**a**).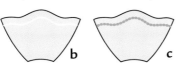

Option B Fuse the fabrics onto the individual patches of interfacing in matching pairs, then use the relevant template on page 76 to mark one side shape on each prepared patch. Cut out the shapes.

2 Use the chalk marker to draw a wavy line roughly 1in below the top edge of each patch, echoing the shape of the wavy edge (**b**). Work a line of machine embroidery along each chalk mark (**c**).

3 Prepare the patch for the bowl base, then use the square centre template on page 76 to mark the shape; cut it out (**d**).

4 Work two layers of satin stitch over the short edges of each side patch (**e**); for this design, don't stitch across the long curve at the top of each patch, or across the bottom edge.

5 Lay the centre shape on a flat surface and arrange the sides evenly around it (**f**); the sides should just touch each other, and will tuck slightly under the edges of the centre. Pin firmly in place.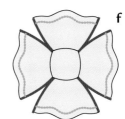

6 Work two circuits of zigzag round the edge of the central shape to secure the side pieces, then trim the bottoms of the side pieces on the back of the work if necessary. Work two circuits of satin stitch round the edges of the centre square (**g**).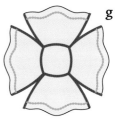

7 Pull the edges of the bowl sides together and join them by hand or machine. Once the sides are joined, trim the tops of the joins level if necessary, then work two circuits of satin stitch all the way around the wavy top edge of the bowl.

TIP Leaving the top edges of the patches till the end creates a smoother outline, and means that you don't have to stitch sharp points at the corners.

Pentagon Flower

Art Deco flowers are often geometric and stylised; I've picked up this idea to design a bowl which is constructed from strong geometric planes, but which creates a flower shape when they're all assembled. The five-sided base and straight sides produce a firm, stable bowl which is also quite capacious.

Difficulty rating ✪ ✪ ✪

Materials

Option A, *if you're making all the sides from the same fabric, as I've done:*

- fusible interfacing:
  for the sides, one 23 x 5½in (59 x 14cm) strip
  for the centre, one 5½in (14cm) square

- fabrics:
  for the sides, two 23 x 5½in (59 x 14cm) strips
  for the centre, two 5½in (14cm) squares

Option B, *if you're making each side in a different fabric:*

- fusible interfacing:
  for the sides, five 4½ x 5½in (11.5 x 14cm) patches
  for the centre, one 5½in (14cm) square

- fabrics:
  for the sides, ten 4½ x 5½in (11.5 x 14cm) patches, two of each colour
  for the centre, two 5½in (14cm) squares

You will also need:

- Contrasting sewing thread

Instructions

1 **Option A** Prepare the strip of interfacing by fusing one strip of fabric to each side. Use the appropriate template on page 77 to mark five side shapes and cut them out in the usual way (**a**).

   Option B Fuse the fabrics onto the individual patches of interfacing in matching pairs, then use the appropriate template on page 77 to mark one side shape on each prepared patch. Cut out the shapes.

2 Prepare the patch for the flower centre, then use pentagon template I on page 94 to mark the shape; cut it out (**b**).

3 Work two layers of satin stitch around the curved edges of the side shapes (**c**); don't stitch across the bottom edges.

4 Lay the base pentagon on a flat surface and arrange the sides evenly around it (**d**); the side pieces should just touch each other, and will tuck slightly under the edges of the centre. Pin firmly in place.

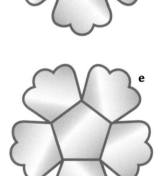

5 Work two circuits of zigzag round the edge of the central pentagon to secure the petals, then trim the bottoms of the petals on the back of the work if necessary. Work two circuits of satin stitch round the edges of the centre shape (**e**).

6 Pull the edges of the sides together and join them by hand to the point marked on the template. (The sides of this bowl are too steep to join by machine.)

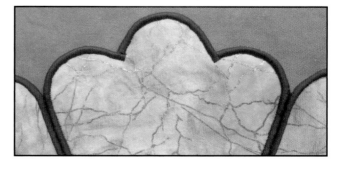

TIP If you'd like to make a smaller bowl using the same shapes, use a photocopier to reduce both templates to 85%.

Asymmetric Pentagon

Geometric planes form angled surfaces in this design and give the finished bowl quite an architectural feel. The side pieces are formed from asymmetric pentagons, stitched around a regular five-sided base. I've used silk dupion in six soft Art Deco pastel colours, and outlined the shapes with a variegated thread in toning shades.

Difficulty rating ✪ ✪

Materials

Option A, *if you're making all the sides from the same fabric:*

- fusible interfacing:
  for the sides, one 21 x 5½in (54 x 14cm) strip
  for the centre, one 5½in (14cm) square

- fabrics:
  for the sides, two 21 x 5½in (54 x 14cm) strips
  for the centre, two 5½in (14cm) squares

Option B, *if you're making each side in a different fabric, as I've done:*

- fusible interfacing:
  for the sides, five 4½ x 5½in (11.5 x 14cm) patches
  for the centre, one 5½in (14cm) square

- fabrics:
  for the sides, ten 4½ x 5½in (11.5 x 14cm) patches, two of each colour
  for the centre, two 5½in (14cm) squares

You will also need:

- Contrasting sewing thread

Instructions

1 **Option A** Prepare the strip of interfacing by fusing one strip of fabric to each side. Use the appropriate template on page 77 to mark five side shapes and cut them out in the usual way (**a**). Use a pin or a dot of pencil to mark the bottom edge of each side shape – it's easy to lose track of which edge is which!

Option B Fuse the fabrics onto the individual patches of interfacing in matching pairs, then use the appropriate template on page 77 to mark one petal shape on each prepared patch. Cut out the petals. Mark the bottom edge of each shape as above.

2 Prepare the patch for the base, then use pentagon template I on page 94 to mark the shape; cut it out (**b**).

3 Work two layers of satin stitch over the short edges of each side patch (**c**); for this design, don't stitch across the pointed edge at the top of each patch, or across the bottom edge.

4 Lay the centre shape on a flat surface and arrange the sides evenly around it (**d**); the sides should just touch each other, and will tuck slightly under the edges of the centre. Pin firmly in place.

5 Work two circuits of zigzag round the edge of the central shape to secure the side pieces, then trim the bottoms of the side pieces on the back of the work if necessary. Work two circuits of satin stitch round the edges of the centre pentagon (**e**).

6 Pull the edges of the bowl sides together and join them by hand; the angles at the base are too steep to join by machine. Once the sides are joined, trim the tops of the joins level if necessary, then work two circuits of satin stitch all the way around the pointed top edge of the bowl; doing the whole top edge in one go like this creates a smoother finish.

TIP The variegated thread I found moves from one colour to another at random intervals, which gives a prettier effect than the ones that are totally regular.

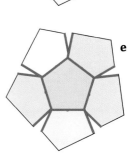

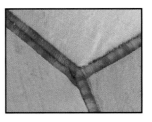

Art Deco Delights: Asymmetric Pentagon

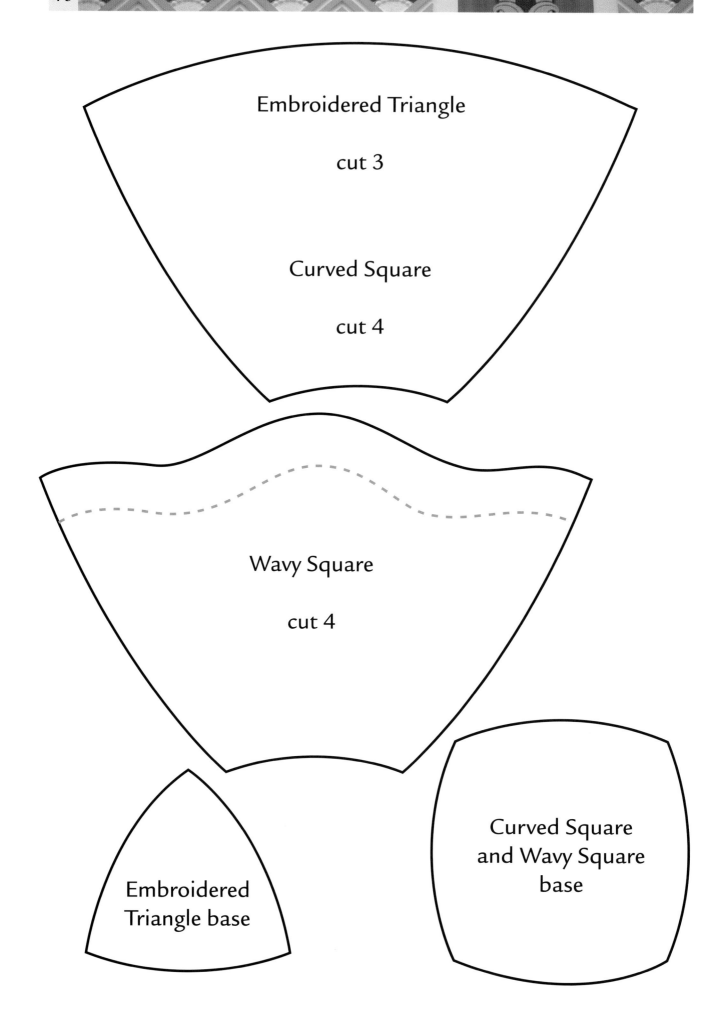

Embroidered Triangle

cut 3

Curved Square

cut 4

Wavy Square

cut 4

Embroidered Triangle base

Curved Square and Wavy Square base

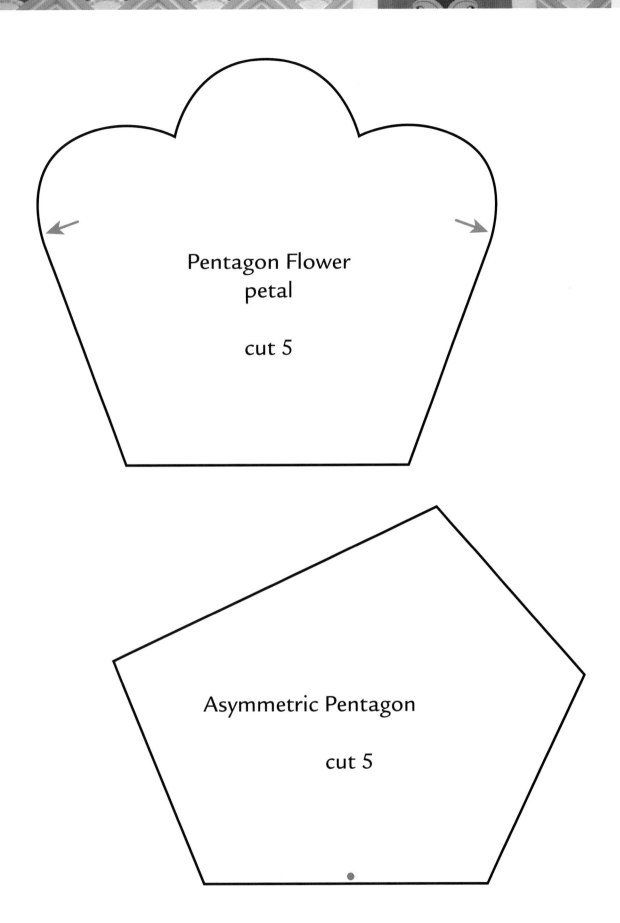

Pentagon Flower
petal

cut 5

Asymmetric Pentagon

cut 5

Kids' Stuff

Children have a legendary ability to collect 'stuff': vitally important bits and pieces that can't possibly be thrown away! Help them to keep those little trinkets and toys organised by making a few bowls; the Bright Flowers and the Long Basket are very roomy, so will hold quite a few priceless treasures …

Bright Flowers

This design cleverly uses the same flower shape to create both the sides and the base of the bowl. It looks particularly striking if you make each flower in a different fabric from a toning range, but would also work very well if you used a single bright batik or hand-dyed fabric for all the flowers.

Difficulty rating ✪ ✪ ✪

Materials

Option A, if you're making all the flowers from the same fabric:

- fusible interfacing:
  one 18 x 12in (46 x 11.5cm) strip
- fabrics:
  two 18 x 12in (46 x 11.5cm) strips of bright fabric

Option B, if you're making each flower in a different fabric, as I've done:

- fusible interfacing:
  six 6in (15cm) squares, two of each fabric
- fabrics:
  twelve 6in (15cm) squares, two of each fabric

You will also need:

- Contrasting sewing thread

Instructions

1 **Option A** Prepare the strip of interfacing by fusing the strips of bright fabric onto it. Use the relevant template on page 85 to mark six flower shapes, and cut them out in the usual way.

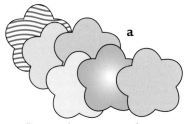

   Option B Fuse the fabrics onto the individual patches of interfacing in matching pairs, then use the relevant template on page 85 to mark one flower shape on each prepared patch. Cut out the flowers (**a**).

2 Work two layers of satin stitch around the edge of each flower shape (**b**). Begin stitching at one of the inner angles of each flower shape.

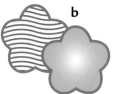

3 Choose one of the flowers to be the base of the bowl and lay it on a flat surface.

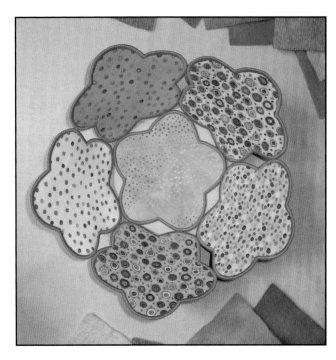

Arrange the other flowers around it, one on each 'side' of the central flower (**c**), then pin firmly in place where the shapes touch.

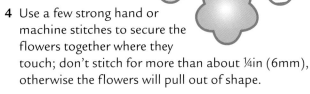

4 Use a few strong hand or machine stitches to secure the flowers together where they touch; don't stitch for more than about ¼in (6mm), otherwise the flowers will pull out of shape.

5 Pull the edges of the flowers together so that the lower petals of the flowers just touch; join by hand or machine as before. Now do the same with the upper petals to complete the bowl.

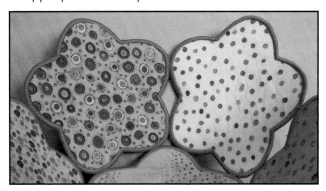

TIP If you'd like a slightly smaller bowl, use a photocopier to reduce the template to 85%.

Rainbow Hexagon

The six sides of this cheery bowl give you the chance to work round the colours of the rainbow; I picked a print fabric in each of the six colours, then edged each one with the next colour in the spectrum. The big central hexagon then gives you a great chance to show off a novelty print in bright colours.

Difficulty rating ✪

Materials

***Option A**, if you're using the same fabric for all the sides:*

- fusible interfacing:
  for the sides, one 26 x 4½in (66 x 11.5cm) strip
  for the base, one 6in (15cm) square

- fabrics:
  for the sides, two 26 x 4½in (66 x 11.5cm) strips
  for the base, two 6in (15cm) squares

***Option B**, if you're making each side of the bowl in a different fabric, as I've done:*

- fusible interfacing:
  for the sides, six 4½in (11.5cm) squares
  for the base, one 6in (15cm) square

- fabrics:
  for the sides, twelve 4½in (11.5cm) squares, two of each fabric
  for the base, two 6in (15cm) squares

You will also need:

- Sewing thread(s) to contrast with the fabric patches

Instructions

1 **Option A** Prepare the strip of interfacing by fusing the strips of fabric onto it. Use the appropriate template on page 84 to mark six side shapes, and cut them out in the usual way.

   Option B Fuse the fabrics onto the individual patches of interfacing in matching pairs, then use the relevant template on page 84 to mark one side shape on each prepared patch. Cut out the shapes (**a**).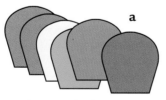

2 Prepare the patch for the base, then use hexagonal template H on page 93 to mark the centre shape and cut it out (**b**).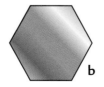

3 Work two layers of satin stitch around the curved edges of the bowl sides (**c**); don't stitch across the bottom edge of the petal shapes.

4 Lay the base shape on a flat surface and arrange the sides evenly around it (**d**) in rainbow order; the sides should just touch each other, and will tuck slightly under the edges of the central hexagon. Pin firmly in place.

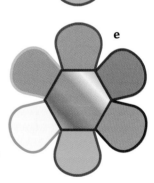

5 Work two circuits of zigzag round the edge of the centre shape to secure the sides, then trim the bottoms of the side shapes on the back of the work if necessary. Work two lines of satin stitch round the edges of the centre hexagon (**e**).

6 Pull the edges of the bowl together and join them by hand to the point marked on the template; you'll find that the sides of this bowl are too steep to join by machine.

TIP If you've used a different-coloured thread for each side of this bowl, pick a totally different one for stitching the edges of the base.

Teddies

An irresistible design; six cute teddy bears play ring-a-ring-a-roses round the edge of this bowl. I made the teddy shapes from a range of toning striped and plaid fabrics, which gives them a sense of unity without them all being the same. You could try them in bright prints – or make them in bear-coloured fabric and add brightly-coloured bow ties.

Difficulty rating ✪ ✪ ✪ ✪

Materials

Option A, *if you're making all the bears from the same fabric:*

- fusible interfacing:
  for the bears, one 26 x 6in (66 x 15cm) strip
  for the base, one 6in (15cm) square

- fabrics:
  for the bears, two 26 x 6in (66 x 15cm) strips
  for the base, two 6in (15cm) squares

Option B, *if you're making each bear in a different fabric, as I've done:*

- fusible interfacing:
  for the bears, six 4½ x 6in (11.5 x 15cm) patches
  for the base, one 6in (15cm) square

- fabrics:
  for the bears, twelve 4½ x 6in (11.5 x 15cm) patches, two of each colour
  for the base, two 6in (15cm) squares

You will also need:

- Contrasting sewing thread
- 24 small, round beads for the eyes, 12 small triangular beads or buttons for the noses, and 12 small ribbon bows for the bow ties, plus matching sewing threads

Instructions

1 **Option A** Prepare the strip of inter-facing by fusing the strips of fabric onto it. Use the relevant template on page 85 to mark six teddy shapes, and cut them out in the usual way.

Option B Fuse the fabrics onto the individual patches of interfacing in matching pairs, then use the relevant template on page 85 to mark one teddy shape on each prepared patch. Cut out the bears (**a**).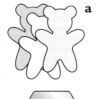

2 Prepare the patch for the base, then use hexagon template H on page 93

to mark the centre shape and cut it out (**b**). Trim each corner very slightly to create a small curve (**c**).

3 Work two layers of satin stitch all around the edges of each teddy (**d**); begin at the top of
the neck on one side (it doesn't matter which one); this will make the beginning and end of your stitching less noticeable. Follow the markings on the template to stitch a double loop of narrow satin stitch on each teddy to create a smile. Stitch on a little triangular bead above each mouth to create a nose, then add two small round beads for the eyes (**e**). Stitch a jaunty bow tie on each side of each bear (**f**).

5 Work two layers of satin stitch all around the edges of the base hexagon. Lay the base on a flat surface and arrange the teddies evenly around it, one on each straight side of the hexagon (**g**), so that the bottoms of their legs just touch the edge. Pin firmly in place.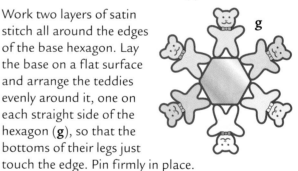

6 Use a few strong hand or machine stitches to secure the ends of the legs to the base where they touch; don't stitch for more than about ¼in (6mm), otherwise the shapes will distort.

7 Pull the sides up into a bowl shape and use the same method to join the legs of the teddies where they touch. Once you've stitched all the joins between the legs, pin the arms together so that they just touch and join in the same way.

Duck-Pond

Yellow gingham ducks swim in a sedate circle round this fun bowl. I've trimmed the base shape to create the impression of a puddle of water, and quilted a watery design to emphasise the effect; if you'd like to make a simpler version you can just use the hexagonal base as it is, or curve the edges slightly as for the Midnight Stars bowl on page 22.

Difficulty rating ✪ ✪ ✪

Materials

***Option A**, if you're making all the ducks from the same fabric, as I've done:*

- fusible interfacing:
  for the ducks, one 18 x 5½in (46 x 14cm) strip
  for the centre, one 6½in (16.5cm) square

- fabrics:
  for the ducks, two 18 x 5½in (46 x 14cm) strips of yellow gingham
  for the centre, two 6½in (16.5cm) squares of blue

***Option B**, if you're making each duck in a different fabric:*

- fusible interfacing:
  for the ducks, five 5½ x 4½in (14 x 11.5cm) patches
  for the centre, one 6½in (16.5cm) square

- fabrics:
  for the ducks, ten 5½ x 4½in (14 x 11.5cm) patches, two of each fabric
  for the centre, two 6½in (16.5cm) squares of blue

You will also need:

- Orange and blue sewing threads
- Ten small round orange beads

Instructions

1 Option A Prepare the strip of interfacing by fusing the strips of yellow fabric onto it. Use the relevant template on page 85 to mark five duck shapes, and cut them out in the usual way (**a**).

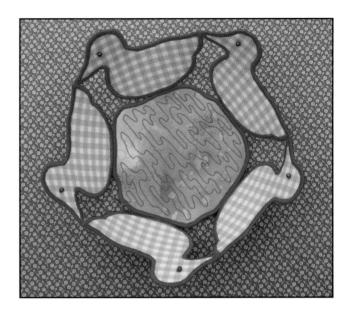

Option B Fuse the fabrics onto the individual patches of interfacing in matching pairs, then use the relevant template on page 85 to mark one duck shape on each prepared patch. Cut out the ducks.

2 Prepare the patch for the bowl base, then use pentagon template J on page 94 to mark the centre shape and cut it out (**b**). Cut the corners of the pentagon into gentle, uneven curves to make the shape look more like a

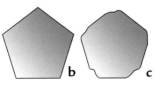

puddle (**c**); don't cut into the edges, as you need these straight so that you can attach the ducks.

3 Use blue thread and free machining to quilt a wavy, watery design on the base (**d**), then work two layers of blue satin stitch all around the edge of the pond shape (**e**).

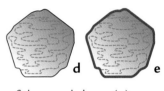

4 Beginning at the tip of the tail, work two layers of orange satin stitch all around the outlines of the duck shapes (**f**). Don't worry if the tail tips aren't very neat when you've stitched them; any rough stitches will be concealed when you join the shapes. (That's why I suggested starting your stitching lines there!) Stitch a little bead to each side of each duck to form the eyes (**g**), stitching them in pairs through each shape; the template shows where these should go.

5 Lay the centre shape on a flat surface and arrange the ducks evenly around it (**h**); pin firmly in place. Use ladder stitch to join the duck shapes to the edges of the pond where the shapes touch.

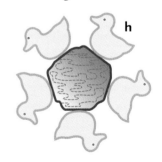

6 Pull the duck shapes up and pin them so that each duck's beak touches the tail tip of the one in front; join them with a few strong stitches by hand or machine.

TIP If you like, you could embroider or appliqué a little wing shape on each duck patch as shown.

Long Basket

A base made from an elongated hexagon produces a nice roomy basket; use bright prints for the sides, and pick a coloured thread that contrasts well. I used a bold stripy print on the inside of the bowl, and found a pretty overall pattern in toning colours for the base and the outsides.

Difficulty rating ✪ ✪

Materials

***Option A**, if you're using just two fabrics for the sides, as I've done:*

- fusible interfacing:
  for the bowl sides, one 14 x 8in (35.5 x 20cm) rectangle
  for the base, one 7 x 4in (18 x 10cm) rectangle

- fabrics:
  for the bowl sides, two 14 x 8in (35.5 x 20cm) rectangles, one of each fabric
  for the base, two 7 x 4in (18 x 10cm) rectangles

***Option B**, if you're making each side of the bowl in a different fabric:*

- fusible interfacing:
  for the long sides, two 4½ x 5½in (11.5 x 14cm) patches
  for the short sides, four 4½in (11.5cm) squares
  for the base, one 7 x 4in (18 x 10cm) rectangle

- fabrics:
  for the long sides, four 4½ x 5½in (11.5 x 14cm) patches, two of each colour
  for the short sides, eight 4½in (11.5cm) squares, two of each colour
  for the base, two 7 x 4in (18 x 10cm) rectangles

You will also need:

- Contrasting sewing thread

Instructions

1 **Option A** Prepare the large rectangle of interfacing by fusing one large rectangle of fabric onto each side. Use the relevant templates on page 84 to mark two long sides and four short ones, following the layout shown (**a**), and cut them out in the usual way (**b**).

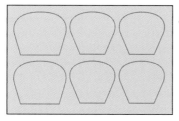

Option B Fuse the fabrics onto the individual patches of interfacing in matching pairs, then use the long and short side templates on page 84 to mark the bowl sides onto the appropriate prepared patches. Cut out the shapes.

2 Prepare the patch for the bowl base, then use the base template on page 94 to mark the hexagon and cut it out (**c**).

3 Work two layers of satin stitch around the curved edges of the bowl sides (**d**); don't stitch across the bottom edges of the shapes.

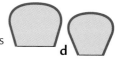

4 Lay the base on a flat surface and arrange the sides around it (**e**); the shapes should just touch each other, and will tuck slightly under the edges of the elongated hexagon. Pin firmly in place.

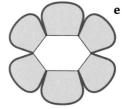

5 Work two circuits of zigzag round the edge of the base to secure the sides, then trim the bottoms of the side patches on the back of the work if necessary. Work two lines of satin stitch round the edges of the centre shape (**f**).

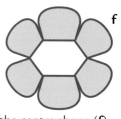

6 Pull the edges of the bowl sides together and join them to the points marked on the templates. If you're careful, it is possible to join the sides by machine; stitch each edge of the long sides first, then join the final seams.

TIP If you're using a directional print, like my stripes, make sure that your fabric strip is large enough, and cut in the right direction, to allow you to cut the bowl sides from the bits you want. If necessary, fuse and cut each patch individually.

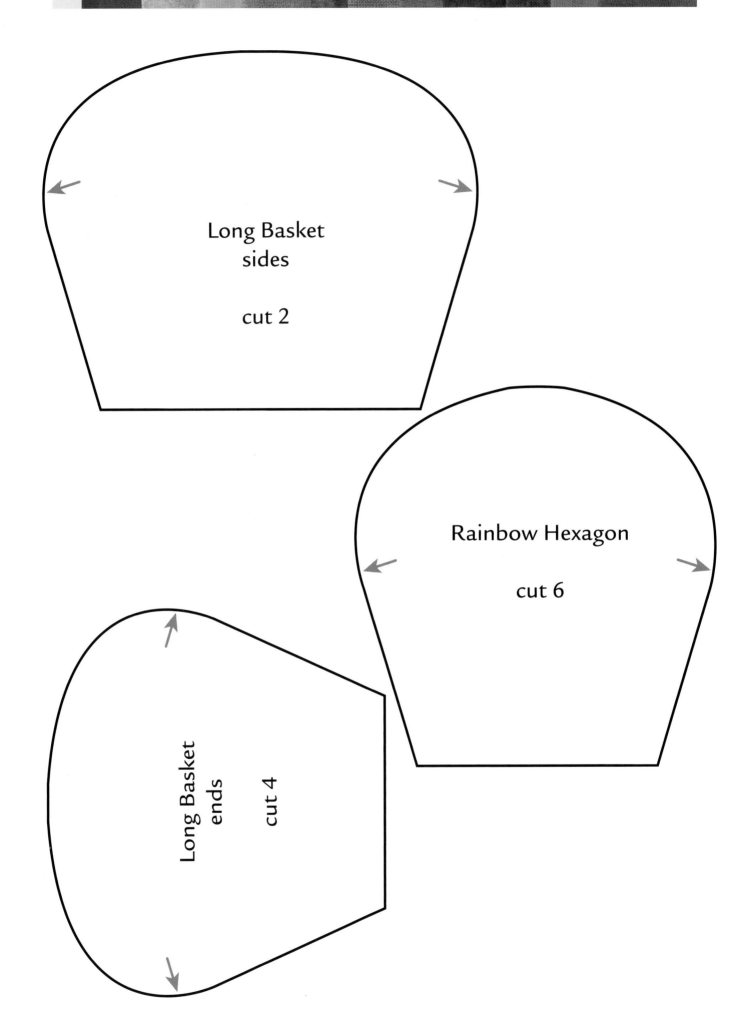

Long Basket
sides

cut 2

Rainbow Hexagon

cut 6

Long Basket
ends

cut 4

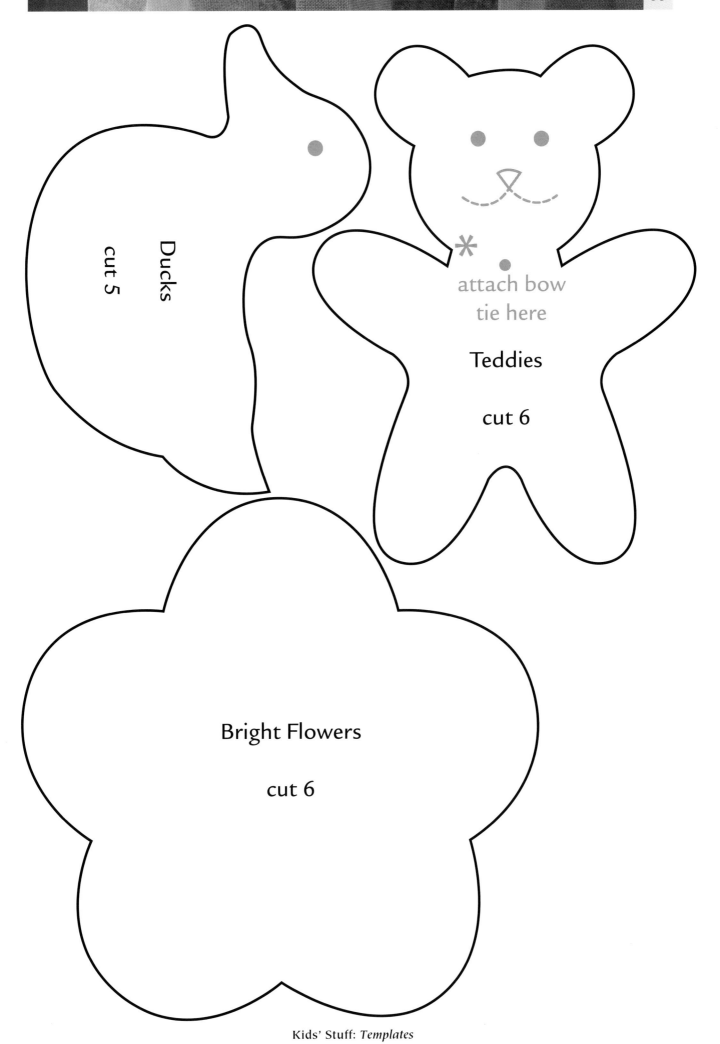

Ducks

cut 5

Teddies

attach bow
tie here

cut 6

Bright Flowers

cut 6

Kids' Stuff: *Templates*

The Exotic Collection

The wonderful fabrics and threads available to stitchers these days give us the opportunity to create real works of art. If you have some exotic scraps left over from special stitching projects, try incorporating them into these intriguing bowls; I've designed them in unusual shapes to flatter the exciting textures of the materials.

Blazing Sun

Yellow and orange batik fabrics are combined with bright stitching in this bowl to create a vivid sunburst design. The rays of the sun are embellished with simple machine quilting in a flame pattern; you could always add red or gold beads or jewels, too, to catch the light and increase the sun's radiance.

Difficulty rating ✪ ✪ ✪

Materials

Option A, *if you're making all the sun's rays from the same fabric, as I've done:*

- fusible interfacing:
  for the arms, one 18 x 5½in (46 x 14cm) strip
  for the centre, one 3in (7.5cm) square

- fabrics:
  for the arms, two 18 x 5½in (46 x 14cm) strips of bright yellow
  for the centre, two 3in (7.5cm) squares of bright orange

Option B, *if you're making each of the sun's rays in a different fabric:*

- fusible interfacing:
  for the arms, eight 2½ x 5½in (6.5 x 14cm) patches
  for the centre, one 3in (7.5cm) square

- fabrics:
  for the arms, sixteen 2½ x 5½in (6.5 x 14cm) patches, two of each colour
  for the centre, two 3in (7.5cm) squares of bright orange

You will also need:

- Dark orange or bright red sewing thread

Instructions

1 **Option A** Prepare the strip of interfacing by fusing one strip of yellow fabric to each side. Use the appropriate template on page 91 to mark eight sun's ray shapes and cut them out in the usual way (**a**).

   Option B Fuse the fabrics onto the individual patches of interfacing in matching pairs, then use the appropriate template on page 91 to mark one sun's ray shape on each prepared patch. Cut out the shapes.

2 Prepare the patch for the bowl's centre, then use the centre template A on page 93 to mark the shape; cut it out (**b**).

3 Use free machine quilting to stitch random flame shapes up the centre of each ray (**c**).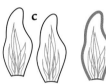

4 Work two layers of satin stitch around the curved edges of the rays (**d**); don't stitch across the bottom edges of the rays.

5 Lay the centre shape on a flat surface and arrange the rays evenly around it (**e**); the rays should just touch each other, and will tuck slightly under the edges of the centre. Pin firmly in place.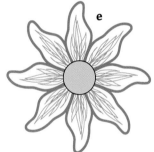

6 Work two circuits of zigzag round the edge of the central shape to secure the rays, then trim the bottoms of the rays on the back of the work if necessary. Work two circuits of satin stitch round the edges of the central circle (**f**).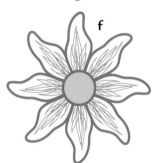

7 Pull the edges of the rays together and join them by machine to the point marked on the template. Don't stitch further than this point, or the bowl will distort.

TIP If you're not confident with free-motion quilting, you could work wiggly lines of straight stitch or machine embroidery stitches to decorate the rays instead.

The Exotic Collection: *Blazing Sun*

Pointed Flower

I've used this pretty flat bowl design to show off two complementary fabrics. I covered one side of the interfacing strip with a subtle batik fabric, overprinted with a design of gold ferns, and picked a silk dupion in a toning colour for the other side. I then used the batik side as the top of three petals, and the silk side as the top of the other three.

Difficulty rating ✪ ✪

Materials

Option A, *if you're making all the petals from the same two fabrics, as I've done:*

- fusible interfacing:
    for the petals, one 24 x 5in (61 x 13cm) strip
    for the centre, one 3½in (9cm) square

- fabrics:
    for the petals, two 24 x 5in (61 x 13cm) strips, one of each fabric
    for the centre, two 3½in (9cm) squares

Option B, *if you're making each petal in a different fabric:*

- fusible interfacing:
    for the petals, six 4½ x 5in (11.5 x 13cm) patches
    for the centre, one 3½in (9cm) square

- fabrics:
    for the petals, twelve 4½ x 5in (11.5 x 13cm) patches, two of each colour
    for the centre, two 3½in (9cm) squares

You will also need:
- Contrasting sewing thread

Instructions

1 **Option A** Prepare the strip of interfacing by fusing one strip of fabric to each side. Use the relevant template on page 91 to mark six petal shapes and cut them out in the usual way (**a**).

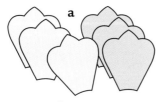

    Option B Fuse the fabrics onto the individual patches of interfacing in matching pairs, then use the relevant template on page 91 to mark one petal shape on each prepared patch. Cut out the petals.

2 Prepare the patch for the flower centre, then use centre template B on page 92 to mark the shape; cut it out (**b**).

3 Work two layers of satin stitch around the curved/pointed edges of the petals (**c**); don't stitch across the bottom edges of the petal shapes.

If you're alternating the fabric on the petals as I've done, remember to use three of the petals with one fabric facing up, and three the other way up.

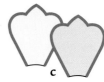

4 Lay the centre shape on a flat surface and arrange the petals evenly around it (**d**), alternating the fabrics around the circle; the petals should just touch each other, and will tuck slightly under the edges of the centre. Pin firmly in place.

5 Work two circuits of zigzag round the edge of the central shape to secure the petals, then trim the bottoms of the petals on the back of the work if necessary. Work two circuits of satin stitch round the edges of the centre (**e**).

6 Pull the edges of the petals together and join them by machine to the point marked on the template.

TIP If you'd like a deeper bowl, trim down the sides of the template slightly so that the sides will be steeper when you join them.

Braided Bowl

Here's something a little bit different: this design is created from a series of geometric sun-ray shapes, but I've joined the rays by pulling them up with a strip of gold braid round the outside. I found a lovely mottled batik to use for the patches, but you could make it in more traditional solar colours, like the bowl on page 87, for a more geometric sunburst. If you don't want to use braid to join the bowl, you could stitch large beads between the rays instead.

Difficulty rating ✪ ✪

Materials

Option A, *if you're making all the rays from the same fabric, as I've done:*

- fusible interfacing:
  for the rays, one 21 x 5½in (54 x 13cm) strip
  for the base, one 3in (7.5cm) square

- fabrics:
  for the rays, two 21 x 5½in (54 x 13cm) strips
  for the base, two 3in (7.5cm) squares

Option B, *if you're making each ray in a different fabric:*

- fusible interfacing:
  for the rays, eight 3 x 5½in (7.5 x 14cm) patches
  for the base, one 3in (7.5cm) square

- fabrics:
  for the rays, sixteen 3 x 5½in (7.5 x 14cm) patches, two of each colour
  for the base, two 3in (7.5cm) squares

You will also need:

- Contrasting sewing thread
- 28in (71cm) braid or ribbon to complement your fabric

Instructions

1 **Option A** Prepare the strip of interfacing by fusing one strip of fabric to each side. Use the appropriate template on page 91 to mark eight ray shapes and cut them out in the usual way (**a**).

Option B Fuse the fabrics onto the individual patches of interfacing in matching pairs, then use the appropriate template on page 91 to mark one ray shape on each prepared patch. Cut out the rays.

2 Prepare the patch for the base, then use centre template A on page 92 to mark the shape; cut it out (**b**).

3 Work two layers of satin stitch around the outside edges of the ray shapes (**c**); don't stitch across the bottom edges of the rays.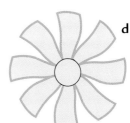

4 Lay the centre shape on a flat surface and arrange the rays evenly around it (**d**); the shapes should just touch each other, and will tuck slightly under the edges of the centre. Pin firmly in place.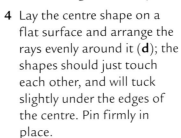

5 Work two circuits of zigzag round the edge of the central shape to secure the rays, then trim the bottoms of the rays on the back of the work if necessary. Work two circuits of satin stitch round the edges of the centre (**e**).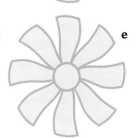

6 Pull the edges of the rays up gently to make a bowl shape. Pin the braid or ribbon round the outside of the rays, making sure that the gaps between the rays are even so that the bowl's symmetrical. Once you're happy with the shape, stitch the braid/ribbon in place by hand on the outside of each ray.

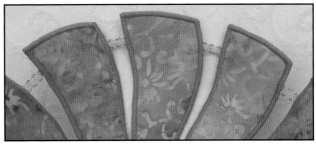

Neaten the raw ends by tying them in a bow, by folding them under and stitching, or by trimming them and covering the ends with a ribbon rose or similar.

Scalloped Flower

This pretty bowl is a variation of the pointed flower design on page 88. I had some lovely embroidered silk dupion left over from a quilt, which gives this bowl almost an Indian feel; you could produce a really rich finish with silk brocade fabric in deep colours, too. Or try a multicoloured batik for a bright, contemporary-looking bowl.

Difficulty rating ✪ ✪

Materials

Option A, *if you're making all the petals from the same fabric, as I've done:*

- fusible interfacing:
  for the petals, one 24 x 5in (61 x 13cm) strip
  for the centre, one 3½in (9cm) square

- fabrics:
  for the petals, two 24 x 5in (61 x 13cm) strips
  for the centre, two 3½in (9cm) squares

Option B, *if you're making each petal in a different fabric:*

- fusible interfacing:
  for the petals, six 4½ x 5in (11.5 x 13cm) patches
  for the centre, one 3½in (9cm) square

- fabrics:
  for the petals, twelve 4½ x 5in (11.5 x 13cm) patches, two of each colour
  for the centre, two 3½in (9cm) squares

You will also need:

- Contrasting sewing thread

Instructions

1 **Option A** Prepare the strip of interfacing by fusing one strip of fabric to each side. Use the relevant template on page 91 to mark six petal shapes and cut them out in the usual way (**a**).

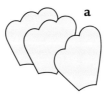

Option B Fuse the fabrics onto the individual patches of interfacing in matching pairs, then use the relevant template on page 91 to mark one petal shape on each prepared patch. Cut out the petals.

2 Prepare the patch for the flower centre, then use the centre template B on page 92 to mark the shape; cut it out (**b**).

3 Work two layers of satin stitch around the scalloped edges of the petals (**c**); don't stitch across the bottom edges of the petal shapes.

4 Lay the centre shape on a flat surface and arrange the petals evenly around it (**d**); the petals should just touch each other, and will tuck slightly under the edges of the centre. Pin firmly in place.

5 Work two circuits of zigzag round the edge of the central shape to secure the petals, then trim the bottoms of the petals on the back of the work if necessary. Work two circuits of satin stitch round the edges of the centre (**e**).

6 Pull the edges of the petals together and join them by machine to the point marked on the template. Don't extend your joining stitches beyond this point, otherwise the petals will distort.

TIP If you'd like a deeper bowl, trim down the sides of the template slightly so that the sides will be steeper when you join them.

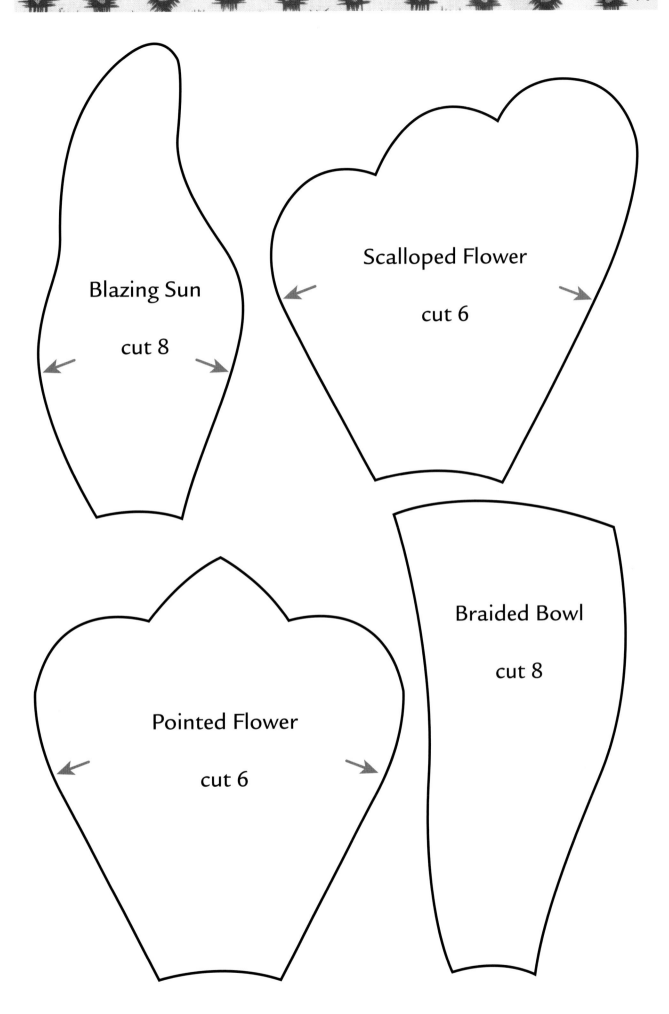

Blazing Sun

cut 8

Scalloped Flower

cut 6

Pointed Flower

cut 6

Braided Bowl

cut 8

The Exotic Collection: *Templates*

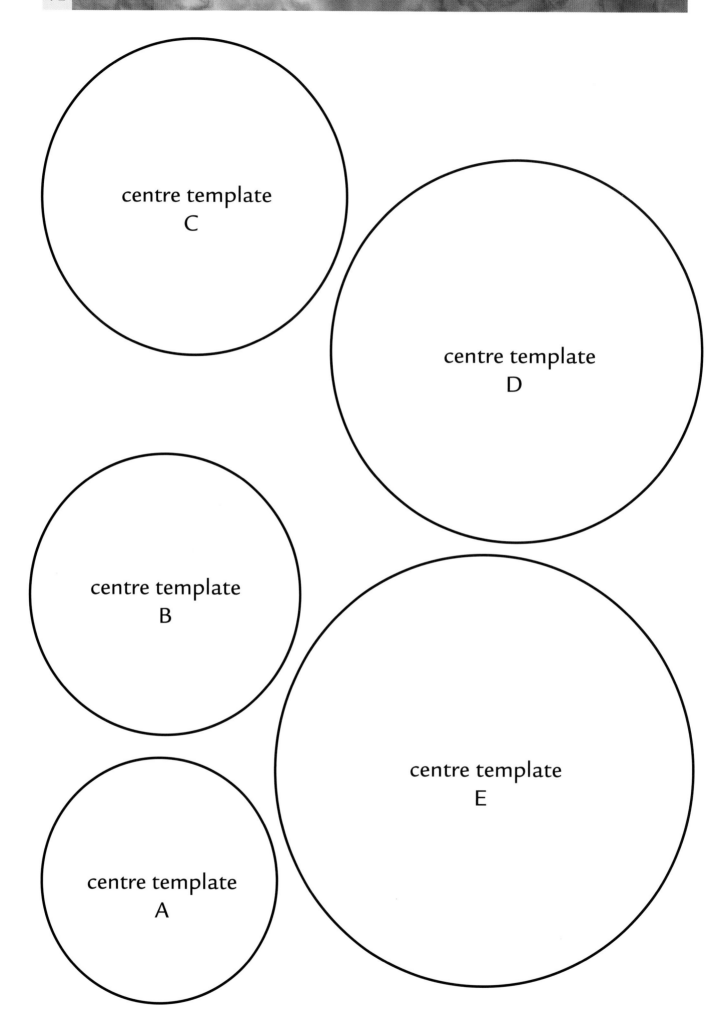

centre template
C

centre template
D

centre template
B

centre template
E

centre template
A

Base and Centre Templates

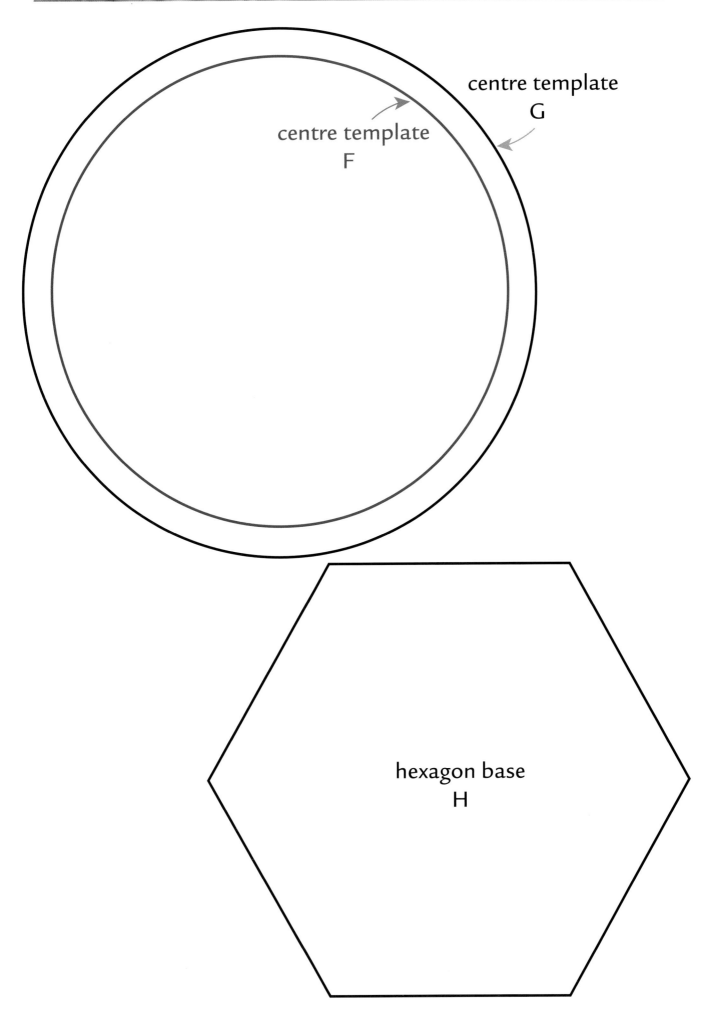

centre template
G

centre template
F

hexagon base
H

Base and Centre Templates

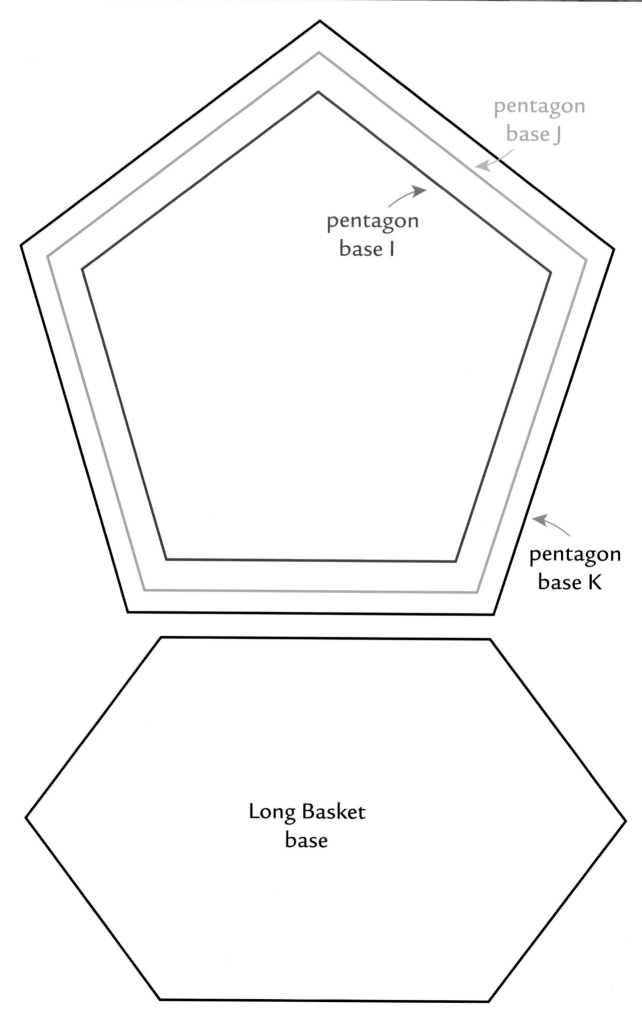

pentagon base J

pentagon base I

pentagon base K

Long Basket base

Base and Centre Templates

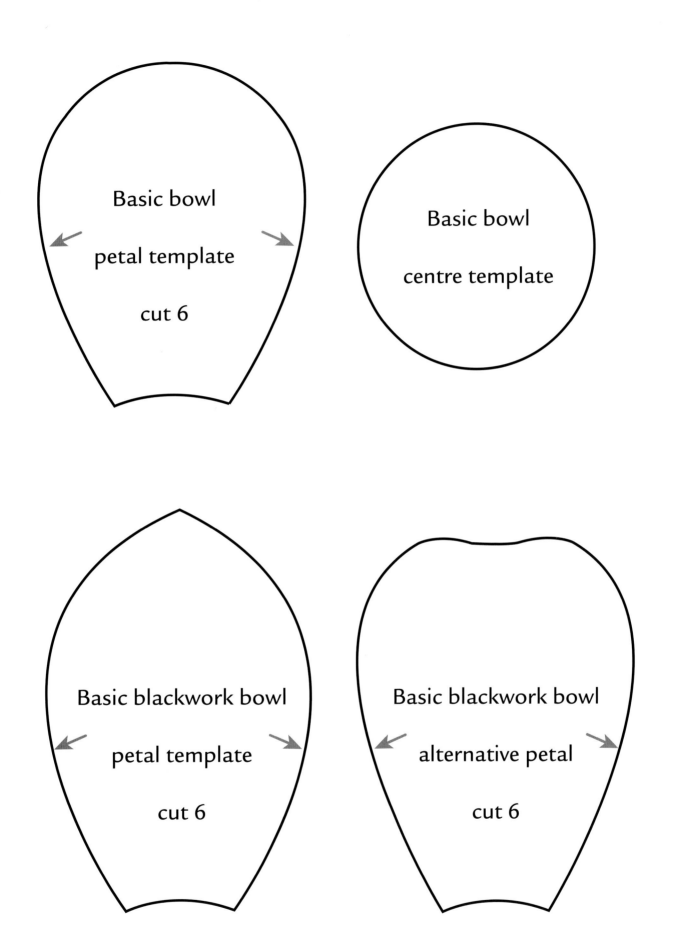

Basic bowl petal template cut 6

Basic bowl centre template

Basic blackwork bowl petal template cut 6

Basic blackwork bowl alternative petal cut 6

Basic Bowl Templates

Contact details

Gail teaches large and small groups of quilters, in all parts of Britian, and abroad. If you'd like to know more about her talks and workshops, or would like details of her other books and stained glass patchwork patterns, contact her in any of the following ways.

post: 44 Rectory Walk, Sompting, Lancing, West Sussex, England BN15 0DU

website: www.gail-quilts-plus.co.uk

e-mail: thelawthers@ntlworld.com

SUPPLIERS

You may find that your local quilt or craft shop stocks Fast2Fuse; if you have difficulty tracking it down, you can order it from the following suppliers:

Kaleidoscope
Cottage Premises
Dobbies Garden Centre
Boclair Road
Milngavie
Glasgow
Scotland G62 6EP
phone: 01360 622 815
website: www.kalquilts.com
e-mail: Kalquilts@aol.com

The Cotton Patch
1285 Stratford Road
Hall Green
Birmingham
B28 9AJ
phone: 0121 702 2840
website: www.cottonpatch.co.uk
e-mail: mailorder@cottonpatch.co.uk